I Feel Better Over Than I Do Anywhere Else

... and Other Stories
to Tickle Your Soul

Randall O'Brien

SMYTH&HELWYS
PUBLISHING, INCORPORATED MACON, GEORGIA

SMYTH &
HELWYS

Smyth & Helwys Publishing, Inc.
6316 Peake Road
Macon, Georgia 31210-3960
1-800-747-3016
©1999 by Smyth & Helwys Publishing
All right reserved.
Printed in the United States of America.
First Edition Copyright© 1996
Second Edition Copyright© 1999

Randall O'Brien

The paper used in this publication meets the minimum requirements of
American National Standard for Information Sciences—Permanence of
Paper for Printed Library Materials.
ANSI Z39.48–1984. (alk. paper)

Library of Congress Cataloging-in-Publication Data

O'Brien, Randall.
    I Feel Better All Over Than I Do Anywhere Else
    . . . and Other Stories To Tickle Your Soul: 2nd edition
    pp.   cm.
    1. Baptists—Sermons. 2. Sermons, American. I. Title.
    BX6333.P67517   1999
    252'.061dc20   95-48119
                                                  CIP
ISBN 1-57312-271-8

I Feel Better All Over Than I Do Anywhere Else

...and other stories to tickle your soul

To my family and friends
who are these stories

Contents

Sin

Death

Quest

Encouragement

Foreword

Imagine a long, serpentine formation leading to the big steel door of endless time. The sentry Archangel listens attentively to each one seeking entry.

"And where did you say you preached?" he asks the man standing at the gate. The man is clutching a big leather-bound, gold-lettered Scofield Bible.

"Firschurch," the candidate replies. Cheerfully.

"I see," says the guardian of heavenly rewards. "And what was it you preached?"

"I preached the pure gospel."

"Please explain."

"I preached fire. I preached banishment. Damnation. Castigation. I preached every Christian a tither. Ten thousand in Sunday School every Sunday. Trot to Training Union. Pack the pews. Buy more buses to bring more tithers to build taller steeples. Praise God! Home and foreign missions. Lottie Moon. A million more in two-o-o-four. I preached what God told me to preach, and He blessed me for it. I preached fire!" There is an uneasy pause. "Uh, but my people never let me stand in lines before," he continues. "Tell Jesus the pastor of Firschurch is here."

"What's that noise back at the end of the line?" the Archangel asks. "Been hearing it all day."

"Oh, just some nut. Believe me, you won't want to talk to him. Says he hasn't brought much to impress you, but he wants in anyhow. Has some silly lil' ole book in his hand. Been yelling the same thing over and over. Name's Randall O'Brien. Known him for years. He's a nut!"

"H'mmm. What's he yelling?"

"Just some gibberish. Childish nonsense. Same thing over and over."

"What's the gibberish? We kind of specialize in nonsense up here."

"No need to bother you with it. I've brought all these from Firschurch for you. Maybe you should just let us all in together."

"But what's he yelling?" the Archangel says, a bit testy himself now.

"He keeps screaming it over and over."

"Screaming what?"

"Well, like I said. He's a nut. He just keeps yelling, 'Grace is trumps! Grace is trumps!! Grace is trumps!!!' "

"Really? You go back there and tell him to come on up front. I won't need to ask him any questions."

And that's what this profoundly serious and scrumptiously funny little volume is all about. Kind of as simple as "you do the hokey-pokey and you turn yourself around, and that's what it's all about."

—Will D. Campbell

GRACE

I Feel Better All Over Than I Do Anywhere Else

Have you ever noticed how Jesus loved to play with our heads? I mean some of the things he said just didn't make sense. For instance, "He who saves his life will lose it; he who loses his life will save it." Or, "The first shall be last; the last shall be first." And "If you wish to become great, become a servant." Or how about, "Happy are those who mourn." Or, "Seeing, they do not see; hearing, they do not hear." And especially this one: "You must be born again."

Folks must have thought him weird. Of course, Jesus was employing paradox to tease us into deeper thought, wasn't he? As the seed of truth germinates within us, watered with the waters of reflection, new spiritual growth might break forth through our crusty souls . . . maybe anyway, perhaps.

Well, methinks God is up to His old tricks again. Into my life from nowhere comes a strange new friend. Known to our family affectionately as "Possum," "Armadillo," or even "Armapossum," believe me, this Possum's different. Lives Alone. Never married. Mows lawns and rakes leaves for a living. That's not what makes him different. You have to hear him talk to understand. Some say he's crazy. Others say he's been in the sun too long. I say he's a national treasure.

One of the first questions Armapossum asked me when we met was, "Is it further to New York City or by bus?" Say what? I'm still working on that one. Then my new friend wanted to know, "Is it hotter in the summer or in the city?" Now, how do you answer that without hurting the man's feelings?

Possum and I get along. Lately, he's been showing up on Sunday nights at the church where I've been preaching. The other night after church we went to get a sandwich and a root beer. He opened up. "I feel more like I do now than I did awhile ago," he shared. I understood.

I confess, some of Armaposssum's revelations take me a little longer. For instance, "Thirty days hath September, April, June, and No Wonder. All the rest eat peanut butter, 'cept Grandma, and she drives a Buick." Hey, gimme time on that one. Once Armadillo came to our home, knocked on the door, and greeted me with this one: "Do you live here, or do you ride a bicycle?" He just wanted to know, I guess.

Possum doesn't want much. Something to eat, roof over his head, a friend—is that too much to ask? Here lately he's begun to tell me more. He's always wanted to be a deacon. Always wanted a wife. Always wanted to sing a solo in church for God. Some things I can help with; some things I can't. Besides, Armapossum is rigid with fear. Still I try.

"Maybe I can help," I allowed. "Now Reverend, you can lead a horse to water, but before you push him in, you'd better think how bad a wet horse smells." "Possum," I related, "it's your call, but if you wanna sing before I preach Sunday night, you can. It's up to you, but I'd like it if you would."

Sunday night came. Armadillo came. Time to sing came. I introduced our guest soloist seated on the back row. Possum froze. Like his nickname's sake, we're talking full body freeze! No pulse. So we rescheduled. When that Sunday arrived, the phone rang. You guessed it: cancellation, again.

Third time's a charm. Are you sitting down? You won't believe it. Guess who just sang "How Great Thou Art" before God and everybody? He did it! He did it! Hallelujah! Possum did it! Like rain falling upon flowers, so his words rained upon our hearts. Innocence and beauty kissed. With Jesus-like wonder, spring decorated our souls. We smiled. We cried. We laughed. We applauded. We repented. We grew.

After everyone had gone, the church building fell silent, dark. Armadillo and I stood outside in the night as families drove away singing. I turned to God's anointed and asked, "Well, how do you feel?" Grinning like a possum eating sawbriars, my friend cried, "I feel better all over than I do anywhere else." . . . You know? So do I.

Mary Nell and Mavis

They went to your school, too. You just called them by some other name. At Netterville Elementary they were called Mary Nell Boatner and Mavis Tapson.

"Oooh, look at the cooties," we mocked piously. "Hey Scag! Where'd you git those cooties?" We'd laugh. Mary Nell Boatner's parents were lowlifers—poor, drunk a lot, lived in the rough part of South McComb. Mary Nell was unkempt —stringy brown hair, plump, squat, green teeth, rotted cavities, clothes old and ragged and hand-me-downs from somewhere. Those who ventured close enough, or were forced to sit by her in class, said she stunk. She was real quiet.

Mavis Tapson was not quiet. She would fight you. She was taller, wild, with red hair. Mavis carried two things in her purse: a red pack of Winstons and a black-handled switchblade. She'd fight you, cut you, cuss you, snarl. So she had to be taunted at a distance—spit and run, whisper in circles.

One day a new kid moved to town—rich kid, good-looking guy. Everybody at Netterville wanted to be his friend. Chris was the strangest kid I ever met. Treated Mary Nell and Mavis like they were people or something. Smiled at them. Called them by name. Junk like that.

We hated Chris. Who'd he think he was anyway? "You coulda been one of the gang, Moneybags," we spewed. "Forget it now, Sucker! Go marry Mavis or Mary Nell!"

When we found out Chris had a year, two at the most, to live—something about some rare disease we didn't understand—we didn't know what to do or how to act around him. He, however, still treated everyone the same with that darned smile of his.

I think we were scared of Chris, everybody except Mavis and Mary Nell. Fact, he's been dead now a long time, and I still might be scared of him—a little anyway, some maybe.

Mary Nell and Mavis? Never the same. Not to themselves. And I guess not to us either. I mean, you couldn't make fun of 'em anymore without thinking of him. And like I said, we never really knew what to do with him. So we just stopped it. All of us.

We all just stopped making fun of people. Stopped being so phony, so pious, so diseased. We all just stopped hating each other. And we began to love like Chris loved. 'Cause we all got cooties. 'Cause ain't none of us got cooties. 'Cause Chris is Christ. And Netterville is now. And this is just a story, but it's the only story there is.

Sewers and Saviors

Seven-year-old Latricia Reese was rescued from raging flood waters that swept her into a Houston, Texas, storm drainage sewer, authorities said, after clinging to a crack in the wall 30 feet under the street for more than 12 hours.

"She spent the entire night in the sewer with all that floodwater coming in on her," said fire department spokesman Mike Warnke. "It's just a miracle she could be alive."

Latricia, who suffered from mild shock, exposure, and some abrasions, plunged several levels underground, twice falling more than six feet before reaching out and clutching a crack in the wall. "I just held onto the crack in the cement," Latricia recalled from her hospital bed hours after her rescue. She said she was bothered throughout by "mosquitoes, ants, and bugs."

"The fire department diving team was called out, and they refused to go in the hole because the water was just so swift that it was too dangerous," Warnke said. "The police diving team was called out, and they refused to go in the hole because the water was just so swift that it was too dangerous," he added.

Latricia was rescued by two construction workers at 8:00 AM the following morning. "We used a flashlight and saw a little figure about 30 feet under the street," one of the workers said. "It was pitch dark, and she couldn't see anything."

How many Latricias would you guess have been swept away by the storms of life? How many of God's precious children are holding on, desperately, to the cracks in the cement? Waters raging at floodstage, swirling overhead! Grip weakening. Time an enemy.

Did not our Savior come to go into sewers? For us! Now who will go in the sewers after Latricia? "Not I," said the fire department. "Not I," said the police department. "Not I," said the preacher. "Not I," said the distinguished churchman. Then who?

Down in Texas, a child of God holding on for life in pitch darkness looked and saw a saving light coming. Construction workers! God uses ordinary people to do God's work. Always has; always will.

Who will pierce the darkness with the light of Christ and find Latricia? Who will go and "give light to those who sit in darkness and in the shadow of death?" (Luke 1:79)

Love Comprehended . . . at Last

Fatherhood: Not until Alyson was born, then Shannon and Christopher, could I fully appreciate God's love for me. Why then? Because of my new perspective. How could a loving father willfully allow the death of his child? For any reason!

Since I love no human enough to sacrifice Alyson, Shannon, or Christopher, it dawned on me. I am that human whom my heavenly Father loves just that much. For God to give His only Son to die for Randall O'Brien could mean only one thing: God loved me beyond my own ability to love or comprehend. So, in not being able to comprehend God's love, and in realizing it, I at last comprehended grace. No other way to put it.

***

Brotherhood: Not until our medical mission trip to Guatemala could I understand how Jesus would be moved to die so that we might live. One might die for his mother or his child, but for countless others?

Then I watched Rudy Jolley practice dentistry, crisis dentistry, with the precious children of Guatemala. Mothers there unknowingly cause massive tooth decay, even eventual abscess, by putting sugar in their babies' milk. It is not uncommon for these little ones to have seven or eight teeth pulled at one sitting. The fear and pain of the shots, along with the extractions, caused some of the children to cry and scream horribly. Something happened to me.

I wanted to take their place, their shots, their abscesses, their pain. I found myself mumbling to no one in particular, "If I could take their place, I would. If it would only make them well."

Seeing children suffer messes with you—big time. Your head, your heart, your soul—it just messes with you. Beats you up emotionally.

If I, a selfish sinner, could be so moved to wish to be a substitute for suffering little ones, then the path Jesus walked makes sense to me. He could take my place and I be well. Take my place and I live. God said he could. Love said he would. Ah, sweet grace ... understood at last.

> *He was wounded for our transgressions, crushed for our iniquities . . . and by his bruises we are healed. (Isaiah 53:5)*

A Kit for All

One cold winter's day I was busily building a fire in our fireplace when Shannon walked up behind me. She was only five. "Daddy, are you a doctor?" she asked. I thought about it for a minute. "Why do you ask, Honey?" I countered, while putting more wood on the fire. "'Cause some people call you Doctor. Allison Payne does." "Well," I conceded, turning to face her, "I guess I am a doctor. I reckon you could say that." "But Daddy, you can't be a doctor," Shannon blurted. "Oh? Why not?" I asked. "You can't be a doctor, Daddy, 'cause you don't even have a kit!"

Shannon is right, of course. Some doctor I am! I don't even have a kit. We often feel so limited to help people who hurt, don't we? I wish I did have a kit, don't you? Know what? If I did have a kit, I know what I'd carry in it: grace. Add love, acceptance, forgiveness, hope, and peace. 'Cause that's what we all need to be well, isn't it?

Shannon is right. I don't even have a kit. But I know someone who does. And, by the way, I have it on good authority this someone still makes house calls. Anytime, anywhere.

All who touched [him] were healed. (Matthew 14:36b)

Super Grace

The drama within the drama snatched our breath. 10, 9, 8 . . . With the final seconds of the Super Bowl clock ticking away, all eyes fall upon one man. With eight seconds remaining, the closest of all Super Bowls will be history. Score? Don't know. Scott Norwood will decide that. With the New York Giants leading 20–19, the Buffalo Bills' kicker runs onto the field to attempt a 47-yard field goal. Make it,

Buffalo wins 22–20. Miss it, and live with it buddy—forever. He misses it. Bills lose. "I let a lot of people down," Norwood cries. "As long as I live, I'll never forget this."

On Monday, January 29, 1991, 25,000 Buffalo fans gathered to welcome their team home. Wildly they cheered their fallen heroes! Then this chant: "We love Scott! We love Scott! We love Scott!" Called to the podium by the fans, Norwood, choking back the tears, with voice breaking, whispered: "I've got to tell you that we're struggling with this right now. I know I've never felt more loved than this right now."

How 'bout it? Have you ever been Scott Norwood? Have so many people counting on you and you blow it? Boy, I have. And don't we struggle with our failures? Memories haunt us. Our guilt grieves us, cruelly. Then this: 25,000 heavenly hosts, Father, Son, and Holy Ghost cheer magnificently. Echoes reverberating throughout the universe, merriment ricocheting off the stars, "We love Randall! We love Randall!" Ah, sweet grace.

What will you remember most about Super Bowl XXV? What I'll remember is not the winning team. New York may have won the game, but the Buffalo fans won my heart. I'll remember them. How warm! How wonderful! Super grace from the Super Bowl. I'll also remember Scott Norwood, that winning player on the losing team. Grace found Scott. Are we not all winners when grace finds us?

And you? Has grace found you? So perhaps you have blown it in front of God and everybody. Close your eyes. Hear the cheers rising from your fans in heaven: "We love you! We love you! We love you!" Did I see a tear?

For by grace you have been saved . . . (Ephesians 2:8a)

Debt Free

Have you ever found yourself in dire need, but absolutely helpless to help yourself? Most of us consider ourselves self-sufficient. We can take care of ourselves. And if not? Then we double our resolve, try twice as hard. "Look out world! Now I'm mad!" But what if nothing works, the dilemma remains, you're still in trouble? Ever been there? I have.

On Tuesday night at 10:45, February 28, 1995, I was returning home after speaking to the Baylor University huddle of Fellowship of Christian Athletes. I noticed my gas gauge was registering empty. Pulling into the nearest convenience store, I filled up my Suburban and then went inside to pay. I could not have known that this store had recently become the target of repeated gasoline-purchase scams. Nor could I have known that it was under police surveillance. And, of course, I did not know that my gasoline credit card had expired.

In a store full of people standing in two parallel long lines before twin registers, I handed my expired credit card to the clerk. Immediately I became the center of attention, both attendants closing in for the kill.

"Do you know your card is expired?" one asked, while the other reached for the phone.

"You're kidding?" I responded.

"Maybe you'd like to pay in cash," one offered in a sarcastic tone.

"I don't have any money with me," I explained. "Can I leave my driver's license with you 'til tomorrow? I'll bring you the $35.00 in the morning." (How could I have known that phony licenses had been used in the scam?)

"Tell it to the police, sir. They're on their way."

I can tell you this. It doesn't feel good to be treated as a con artist, to have a store full of people stare at you in disgust. So I pled, "Can I call my wife?"

"Call who you want. Call the president if you like. Call your mother. Won't do you no good."

I dialed home, beginning to feel desperate. No answer. I tried again. Six, seven rings. Nothing. Two police cars rushed onto the scene. How helpless I was feeling.

The clerk at the distant check-out register complained, "You can go. Forget it."

"What?" I asked.

"You can go. That man paid for your gas."

"What man? Who? Where? What are you talking about?" Looking around the store, I saw no friendly face.

"That man out there getting in his car," he snapped.

Dashing out the door, I managed to catch the man as he prepared to drive away. "Sir, just a minute. Please, who are you?"

"I'm a Christian," he replied. "Don't worry about it. Thank God, not me."

"I do thank God. But I want to thank you, too. What's your name?"

"My name's Bobby Williams. I believe God puts us in situations to help. You sure looked like you could use a little help."

"Look," I answered, "can I have your address? I want to pay you back."

"God already has, my friend," he shared.

"What do you mean?" I asked.

"My son has spina bifada. He's paralyzed from the waist down. Christians have loved Benjamin and prayed for him day and night. Our bills and our suffering, well, it's been hard. Real hard. We know what it's like to need help. Christians have helped us. We're even debt free. I just wanted to help someone else the way others have helped us." With that he smiled and drove away.

Do to others as you would have them do to you.
(Matthew 7:12a)

Back to School

It didn't have a thing to do with school. It wasn't because I didn't wanna leave the nest just yet, although I didn't. It wasn't walking every day from 910 Bendat Street to Netterville Elementary on Beech Street. Half-a-mile's nothing, even for a six-year-old. And it sure wasn't Miss Leblanc, my first grade teacher, because I liked her. Like I said, it didn't have anything to do with school.

What I hated about first grade was Ronald Boyd! He was in elementary school when I got there, and he was in elementary school when I left. The creature was 6'1". To me he was. Makes no difference; he may have been only five-feet tall. He was six-feet tall to me. Ronald was tall, skinny, and mean. Also he was ugly. It was the mean part I hated. The other stuff I figured he didn't volunteer for.

Every day I would walk all 3'7" and 49 pounds of my timid first-grade self to school. And every day Ronald Boyd would walk behind me stepping on my heels with his cowboy boots while he beat me across the head with a rolled-up newspaper.

I hated Ronald Boyd. I used to leave early for school intentionally, except when I would leave late intentionally. No matter; Ronald would wait. Or rise early, skip breakfast, whatever it took—anything to hit my head with his newspaper.

I hated Ronald Boyd. For years I could still see his greasy black comb in his blue jeans back pocket, his Butch hair wax glistening too thick in his flat-top haircut, his tall-heeled cowboy boots with the pointed toes, his evil lanky walk, and of course that rolled-up newspaper.

One cruel difference between memories and actual events, I have discovered, is that memories can humiliate you over and over. Ronald gets to hit your head nightly, while he sleeps, but you don't. "Now I lay me down to sleep . . ." Bam!

What about you? Remember your first bully? Still hate the sucker? I can relate. Then I realized something.

We all walked behind Jesus stepping on his heels ... on purpose pushing him down, humiliating him, mocking him, hitting his head with a rolled-up newspaper. We all did, laughing, and sometimes we still do.

Only his memories aren't like my memories. "Father, forgive them; for they do not know what they are doing" (Luke 23:34). His thoughts are not like my thoughts. "If you forgive others their trespasses, your heavenly Father will also forgive you; but if you do not forgive others, neither will your Father forgive your trespasses" (Matt 6:4-5). . . . Back-to-school time for me, I confess.

Love your enemies and pray for those who persecute you. (Matthew 5:44)

Rehabilitating Randall

Riddle: What do dentures, diets, and disease . . . crowns, cuffs, and cantankerous cartilage have in common?
Answer: They all live in the same neighborhood . . . namely, me!

Okay, I'll admit it. I don't like to, but I will—just this once at least. "The ol' gray mare, she ain't what she used to be." Simply (but painfully) put: I'm aging.

My dentist tells me to go ahead and learn to pronounce "per-i-o-don-tal." He's talking surgery, crowns, dentures, you name it! Just kinda grins and intones, "Gotta be true to your teeth, or they'll be false to you."

Next my doctor informs me I'm overweight . . . all in the gut! Plus, my orthopedic surgeon laughs at my left thigh, which is one inch smaller than the right due to internal derangement of my left knee, skimpy cartilage, or whatever.

Then there's the rotator cuff in my right arm. It's messed up, of course. Causes pain for throwing motions and has caused atrophy of the right bicep. Even a visit to my optometrist recently prompted this impish assessment: "You're going to love your new glasses. We're gonna help you to see again, Ol' Man."

Back to the dentist. He consoles me by saying, "If the oral surgeon doesn't get you, the orthodontist will." And then, to top it all off, sitting in my barber's chair, I am comforted with these words: "If you will massage your scalp every day, you may be able to stop your hair loss." "Hair loss? I didn't know I had any hair loss!" I aggressively responded. "Oh yeah. Big time! Right here in the back. A crown we call it. Then, of course, you're receding there in the front, too." "Thank you. How much do I owe you for the diagnosis," I replied. "On the house," he grinned. "On the house."

Well, I say it's no grinning matter. I'm aging, and the world should be a little more sensitive to my poor aching ego, a little more respectful to an old man's dilapidated body. Just think! Not yet 47 and staring at a lifetime of rehabilitating Randall. Woe is me.

Consolation? Well, yes, I guess there is. The O'Brien-Tyson fight is off. Kay loves me just the way I am. My eyes are going, too, so I don't have to see how bad I look. Finally, there is consolation for all of us aging humans:

His delight is not in the strength of the horse, nor his pleasure in the speed of a runner; but the Lord takes pleasure in those who fear him, in those who hope in his steadfast love. (Psalm 147:10-11)

The Last Word (and the Next-to-Last)

*There is a familiar old maxim which assures us that man
is the noblest work of God. Who found that out?*

—*Mark Twain*

On October 1, 1950, Charles Schultz introduced us to our-
selves. He did so with a cast of cartoon characters led by
Charlie Brown, Linus, and Lucy. In one cartoon Linus asks
Lucy, "When you get big, do you want to be somebody great?"
Lucy responds indignantly: "That's an insult!" "An insult?" asks
Linus, taken aback. Smugly, Lucy, scoffs: "I feel that I'm great
already!"

Ah, don't we bask in the warmth of our own greatness and
strut in the stature of our nobility? So "man is the noblest work
of God? Who found that out?"

Certainly, we would not want to create a colony of self-
despising, self-flagellating beings. Nor should we Christians, on
the other hand, be as eager as Lucy might be to give up the bib-
lical doctrine of the Fall. For, as goes the fall of man, so go the
incarnation and redemption, bedrock doctrines of Christianity.
Put simply: no sin, no Savior.

The good news, as we know of course, is that the final word
with Christ is not guilt, but grace. Yet, Dietrich Bonhoeffer once
reminded us, "You cannot and must not speak the last word
before you have spoken the next-to-last."

So . . . we're great, are we? I'm afraid Lucy's thinking repre-
sents our own. Who needs to grow up to become great? Who
needs Christ? Hey, aren't we great already? Wasn't it Luther who
said, "The ultimate proof of the sinner is that he does not know
his own sin."

Once Schultz said of Lucy, "Perhaps if you scratched deeper,
you'd find she's even worse than she seems." Hmmm. That's us
alright—all of us, I suspect—proudly projecting our greatness
on the surface, but beware of scratching deeper!

Here's to all of us. Two final words. The next-to-last word:
guilty.

For I know that nothing good dwells within me, that is, in my flesh. . . . For I do not do the good I want, but the evil I do not want is what I do. . . . Sin dwells within me. . . . Wretched man that I am! Who will rescue me from this body of death? (Romans 7:18-20, 24)

The last word: grace.

To you is born this day . . . a Savior, who is the Messiah. (Luke 2:11)

Bite the Wax Tadpole

Get this. Coca Cola has changed the name of its soft drink in China. After discovering that the word means, in Chinese, "Bite the wax tadpole," the company thought a change might be in order. The new name translates better: "May the mouth rejoice."

Methinks it's a shame when words lose their meaning in translation. Remember when Christian meant Christian? Alas, now it seems the term is, more often than not, angrily translated into "conservative" or "liberal" or fundamentalist" or "moderate."

Jan is an ordained Southern Baptist minister. She is a graduate of Yale Divinity School and has served as campus minister at Yale and in pastoral roles in the local church. She is an open, honest, warm, and caring person. Jan is a free thinker. Her theology by some notions might be called "liberal."

On the other hand, based on some standards in religious life, Keene is a staunch conservative, a "fundamentalist," as some say. He attended Mid-America Seminary, a zealously conservative bastion of orthodoxy. Whereas Jan is open to new interpretations of Scripture, Keene is a "defender of the faith." He is intelligent, honest, warm, and caring.

Jan and Keene are the Reverend and Reverend Carruthers. Yes, they are married! What a model—for all of us—of love, patience, understanding, commitment! I asked them one evening, "How in the world is this possible?" They replied in unison, "We laugh a lot."

Don't you just love it! Who says unity must mean uniformity? Seems to me Jan and Keene's kind of Christianity translates, "May the mouth rejoice!" Brand X Christianity, on the other hand, i.e., the vicious judgmental variety, is best translated, "Bite the wax tadpole."

Do not judge . . . (Matthew 7:1)

Theology under the Tent

Parenting is great fun . . . until the children are born. Then it gets tough. But we learn a lot.

When our first child came into the world, I was there . . . amidst the primal screams, plastered on the ceiling, drunk on adrenaline, outta my mind. Beholding the most beautiful creation coming into the world, I shouted, "Honey, it's a boy! It's a boy!"

The doctor laughed and said, "Mr. O'Brien, that's the umbilical cord."

"Yeah, yeah, I knew that," I blushed. "Let me hold her, Doctor. Honey, it's Alyson. Let me hold her, Doc."

"Mr. O'Brien, do you mind if we cut the umbilical cord first?"

"No, no, sure, go ahead, Doc."

Soon we were holding Alyson. On-the-job parenting began. Trial and error—lots o' errors, lots o' trials—for instance, potty-training.

One evening while Kay was preparing dinner, Alyson and I were busy playing under a makeshift tent in the den. We were hiding and giggling—"bonding," they call it—under the sheet-and-chair tent, when Alyson whispered, "Mommy can't see us now."

"That's right," I agreed, "Mommy can't see us now."

We played on. What fun, hiding and laughing under the tent; father-daughter, just the two of us.

"Nobody can see us now," Alyson giggled.

"That's right, Honey. No one can see us now," I smiled. We played on.

Yet again, she stopped and pondered, "Mommy can't see us now."

"That's right, Honey. Mommy can't see us now," I assured her.

A long pause . . . "Let's tee-tee."

Think about it. How flattering that my young daughter would trust me. The biggest "no-no" in her life, and she trusted me not to condemn her! "She sees me as love not law," I thought. "She actually sees me as her friend." My heart melted. So I said, "Okay." A pleasant little expression spread over her face as she relaxed and looked into my eyes, and "tee-teed" under the tent.

I learned some good theology that day in our den. Alyson showed me what true trust is, what it means to rest in the Father's unconditional love and acceptance, to breathe the fresh air of assurance. The Bible says we've all "tee-teed" under the tent. Our Father sees and loves us anyway. Ah, sweet grace.

> *There is therefore now no condemnation for those who are in Christ Jesus. (Romans 8:1)*

LOVE

Alex and His Dad

Four-year-old Alex Smith has a hero: his dad. Officials at the Royal Chitwan National Park Wildlife Preserve in Nepal said that Alex was saved by "one of the greatest acts of bravery" they had ever witnessed. His father, Dr. Smith, a professor of fisheries and wildlife at the University of Minnesota who had been studying small mammals in Nepal, was setting up traps near camp when he looked up and saw a huge male rhino charging his son.

"I rushed towards Alex to pull him away, but there was no chance, so I rushed towards the rushing rhino," Dr. Smith said. "I tried to tackle the rhino, and twice I was over him, catching his head. I was probably gored about 14 times in 30 seconds." He received severe chest, leg, and head injuries in the attack.

While Alex's dad was repeatedly pierced by the rhino, two others managed to pull young Alex to safety. "This was one of the greatest acts of bravery. He just stood in front of the charging rhino," one official reported. "And nothing happened to the child."

So what d'ya think? Reckon Alex is proud of his dad? Reckon dad is relieved that his son is safe? Interesting, but macho wildlife rangers like to call this kind of act "bravery." Betcha one day Alex calls it something else. Betcha one day he calls it "love." Know what I call it? A parable. Think about it.

Quills or Quilts?

Psychologist Bruno Bettelheim made an interesting observation. He noted that the German philosopher Schopenhauer once compared the human predicament to two porcupines trying to survive a cold winter.

"To keep from freezing to death, the porcupines hole up in a cave. Because it is very cold even in their cave, they seek warmth and creature comfort by drawing closely together. But the closer they come to each other, the more they prick each other with their quills. Bruised and annoyed, they draw widely apart to avoid pricking each other."

"Alas, now they lose all the comfort and warmth they can give each other and are again threatened with dying of cold. So once more they draw closer together. Eventually, as they move back and forth, they learn to live with each other so that neither is pricked badly, but they are still close enough to live in reasonable comfort."

"This suggests," Bettelheim said, "that we must learn to live close together without getting under each other's skin. If we fail to learn this, we are either too close for comfort, or we freeze emotionally in isolation."

So life is like that? Yes, I suppose it is. But if I understand the work of Christ correctly, his loving desire is to convert porcupines into lambs—to replace quills with quilts, bruises with blankets, muggings with huggings, wounds with warmth. "Brethren, let us love one another," he says.

> You might say he took the wounds
> that we might have the warmth.
> A lamb in a porcupine patch,
> yet his blood gave birth.
> For where it fell on hearts of porcupines,
> lambs were born.
> And those lambs embrace porcupines
> today, as he did then,
> hoping to see new birth.

Until all God's creation
no more be pierced by painful pricks,
but be warmed
by woolen blankets.

The choice, of course, remains ours. New birth or old? Salvo or salve? Quills or quilts? And you, how have you chosen?

How can one keep warm alone? (Ecclesiastes 4:11b)

Catchin' Fish and Catchin' On

Dad would get off work at the *McComb Enterprise-Journal* at 4:00 every afternoon. I'd watch for him. He was a printer at the town newspaper, and I was plenty proud of him.

I could hardly wait! I knew Pa was ready. My grandpa, or "Pa," as we called him, already would have walked home from the McComb water plant where he worked, gotten his fishing pole out from under the house, put his hat on, and be sittin' out on the porch waitin' for us, pullin' out his pocket watch every now and then lookin' at the timepiece that he boasted kept "railroad time."

I could hardly wait! Going' fishin with Daddy and Pa! What could be better 'n that? When Dad would get home, us men would decide, like we always did, then tell Mom, what kind of sandwiches we wanted to take fishin' with us. It was always pimento n' cheese with mayonnaise and tomato—less we were outta pimento. Then it was just mayonnaise and tomato sandwiches. Mother always made an extra one for Pa.

One afternoon Daddy, Pa, and me were fishin' hard at the I. C. Lake. We had fished all afternoon. No luck, not for me anyway. Daddy and Pa, now they knew how to do it. Catchin' a fish is a pretty big deal when a boy's tryin' to be a man. Men notice those things. Women too. Womenfolk'd always ask when you'd get home, "How many'd you catch?" Pa and Daddy were men. And I was trying hard to be. No fish for me this day, though, again. Pa and Daddy were thirsty. They said, "Son, here, take this money and run across the way over there to Welch's Grocery and get us all a soda pop." "But what about my pole?" I protested. "We'll watch it for you. Now hurry."

It wasn't long after returning with Nu Grapes and RC Cola that I noticed it. My cork was underwater! "I got one! I got one!" I screamed. Then with the skill of a real man, with Dad and Pa watching, I landed one of the biggest fish you ever saw. Well, so it mighta been kinda small. I had me one nonetheless. You bet I did, one I could take home and show off. Years later I found out something. I didn't catch that fish. Pa and Daddy put that fish on my pole while I was at Welch's Grocery. Why? 'Cause they loved me.

Today, in a lot of ways I'm still a little boy fishing in McComb, still gloating over the fish I caught. Nice home, great family, wonderful church, material blessings, loving friends, good health, happines . . . And you? Any chance you're basking in "fine, large cities that you did not build, houses filled with all sorts of goods that you did not fill" (Deut 6:10-11)?

Been fishing with your heavenly Father lately? Been to Welch's Grocery? "Do not say to yourself, 'My power and the might of my own hand have gotten me this wealth'" (Deut 8:17). . . . Little children, guess who put that fish on your pole?

Daddy Shall Sleep with the Lamb

It was Friday night late, 10:30 or so. I was packing. Last minute for Guatemala mission trip. In walked a beautiful little brown-eyed brunette, seven years of age with sad eyes. Clutching her stuffed lamb, she watched quietly.

"Hun, what are you doing up?" I asked.

"I couldn't sleep," she whispered. "Daddy?"

"Yes, darling."

"Do you want to carry my lamb with you?"

I stopped what I was doing. There are times when a man becomes a daddy and stops what he's doing.

"Do you want me to carry your lamb, Hun?" I asked gently.

"Well, it would remind you of me, Daddy."

From August 18 to August 25, 1990, every night for one week, for the first time in 33 years—let the record show—your friend, Shannon's daddy, slept with a stuffed lamb. To my surprise, the other six men on our mission trip never kidded me about it. Not a word. Which tells me I'm not the only man in our church who knows when a man should be a daddy.

Jesus loves the little children. . . .

Dear Mother

I don't believe you've heard these words before, and I know you have never read them. Maybe it's that after 46 years some things are just easier to say. Or maybe it's just that as one grows older, he wants to say some things he's never said before. I'm not sure.

Anyway, thank you. That's all. Thank you for bringing me into this world when you yourself were only 20 years old. Thank you for loving me. I used to think all those old stories were corny about how we were so poor you had to pull out a dresser drawer to use for my bed. Now that I'm a daddy I realize how hard it must have been back then—the sacrifices, the struggles.

I remember how you used to stay up with me all night long when I was sick, even though you had to work at the factory all day long the next day. You never complained. Even now I can't remember who hurt worse when I was sick, me or you. Maybe you couldn't make me well, but you sure made it better just by being there. I was never alone. Thanks, Mother.

For nearly 40 years now you have gotten up at 4:30 or 5:00 AM to head off toward the factory. Even today you still make minimum wage, but I don't. You sacrificed so that Sue, Faye, and I could get an education. We've all got good jobs, but nobody seems to like theirs more than you. That's the way you are. And I love you for it.

Remember how you used to slip me $5.00 as I was going off to college? I hated to take it so bad, but loved you so much I did. Not everybody will understand what I'm saying. Turning down the money would have been turning you down. Taking it was taking a part of you with me. How important it was, for both of us.

By the way, I figured you out early on about the apple pie and fried chicken thing. After we all had a slice of pie or piece of chicken at suppertime and just enough remained for everybody but one person to have seconds, you "never really liked apple pie anyway." Thank you for being you, Mother.

I remember how you cried as you saw me off for Vietnam. I carried that picture with me through the war, and life. Thanks for the love.

To this day when people ask me when I first loved Jesus as my Savior, I have to answer: "I can't remember when I didn't." My earliest memories are of your praying with me "Now I lay me down to sleep; I pray the Lord my soul to keep. . . ." How can I ever thank you enough for my love for Jesus?

I could write forever, Mother. How special you are! Guess I just wanted to write to say "Happy Mother's Day." Please know that I think God gave me the greatest mother ever! You've influenced me in more ways than anyone could ever possibly know. But I know.

There is just one area of influence in which you failed, however. Despite the best example a boy could ever have. I still love apple pie and fried chicken. Guess a man just can't ever be a mother.

I love you Mother.

🐝 🐝 🐝

A Son's Love

I am an average athlete. Mediocre. Capital M. There, I said it. Only took me 40-something years to admit it. I hate it! No, not that it took me so long. But I hate being average! Since I am, I'm trying to "get in touch with my true self," "accept my limitations," "be real." It ain't working. Midlife crises don't help. Some unidentified malfunctioning hyperactive gland made me decide to run a marathon this year. I hate unidentified malfunctioning hyperactive glands. My wife says, "There are worse things you could do with your midlife crisis. Go run!"

So I ran. Average. Of course. On December 10 somehow I survived the Honolulu Marathon—89° heat, 84% humidity, 26.2 miles. Hotter 'n Helsinki. Josiah Thungwanbe, a South African, won the race in 2 hours and 16 minutes. He and I had identical times. Except I had 13 miles to go. Finishing in 4 hours isn't exactly world-class. But, hey, it beats death, which I had thought might come before the finish line.

All finishers received medals. Along with 27,000 others, no less, I got one, too. My family was so proud; you'd have thought I won. Recently Christopher, my seven-year-old son, had some friends over to play. As they played in his room, I overheard him boast, "My dad can run 20 miles." My world stopped. Stood still. I listened. "Hey Adam, Richard, know what? My dad can run 20 miles." My heart melted. I wanted to whisper, "26.2 miles to be exact, Chris."

In a few moments, the boys burst out of the room running outside to play. Around Christopher's neck, swinging to and fro, bouncing as he ran, hung my marathon medallion. Chris was wearing my medal! I teared up. Average ol' me loved incredibly by my son!

Lately, ol' you-know-who is rediscovering a newfound joy: praising to others my Father in heaven. Hardly average that race he ran in flesh 2,000 years ago, would you say? Funny. I've taken that old cross necklace out of the dresser drawer. And . . . I'm wearing his medal.

> . . . Let us run with perseverance the race that is set before us, looking to Jesus. . . who for the sake of the joy that was set before him endured the cross . . . (Hebrews 12:1-2)

They Love Me. . . . They Love Me Not

Being a pastor is a perilous profession. Perilous not because we're prophets, a phenomenon of days bygone, 'cause we're not. We wanna be liked much too much for that.

"Prophets for profit," some have said. But they're wrong, too. Tain't so. Not really anyway. Money is nice. Sure. But as four British youths from Liverpool once sang, "Money can't buy me love." Neither prophet nor profit factors make pastoring perilous. Pastoring is perilous 'cause we wanna be popular.

Pastors are people. No one said that, but somebody should. Like other humanoids, we hurt. We cry. We laugh. We love. We wanna be loved.

Giving is up. . . . They love me. Sermon was too long. . . . They love me not. Visited Aunt Nellie. . . . They love me. Missed the social. . . . They love me not. Attendance is up. . . . They love me. Budget is tight. . . . They love me not. Preached short. . . . They love me. Business meeting was tense. . . . They love me not. They love me. . . . They love me not.

Ever felt that way? About your life, significant relationships, your gang, your church, friends, casual acquaintances? "They love me. . . . They love me not." Wonder if God ever feels that way about us?

. . . These people draw near with their mouths and honor me with their lips, while their hearts are far from me. (Isaiah 29:13a)

Sharon-Share-Alike

Sharon shared her love freely. All the boys called her Share-and-share-alike, or Sharon-share-alike. Maybe you remember Sharon from your high school days. Every high school has a Sharon. And every high school has a guy like me: messiah complex, feel sorry for everybody, save the world, save Sharon.

Beats me why I was drawn to Sharon. Not for the same reasons others bragged about in the locker room. I dunno why. She was cute. Sharon just tried too hard. But then, so did I. Maybe I'm the one who needed saving. Anyway, no one really liked Sharon. Least not the way she wanted to be liked.

Sharon never knew I was alive. She was a cheerleader. The girls said she "bought" her votes. I was too skinny for football, too slow for track, couldn't hit a curve ball, tennis was for sissies Daddy said, so out I went for basketball. How could I win Sharon's love, if she didn't know I existed? Basketball it was.

That first year of basketball? In a word? Hades. I was so skinny, I could walk through a harp. Everyone would snicker, "Hey, O'Brien, are those your legs, or are you riding a chicken?" "Hey everybody, here comes O'Brien. Move the Coke bottles. He'll step in one and break his leg." Alas, they were right. How many times did I hear, "Hey, O'Brien, you're so skinny, you only have one stripe on your pajamas!"

Life was hard. Basketball, impossible! Spastic! I was so spastic, I tripped on the lines on the court. Maybe Sharon would at least notice me. But second team, junior varsity? Hope springs eternal.

The day came to get our team uniforms. I raced to the table on the sidelines without falling. Got the number I wanted. Coach said, "Not so fast, O'Brien. Put that back. Get in the back of the line." Woe is me. Got the last pair of pants left. You shoulda seen 'em. I coulda played in one leg. Fat Albert woulda had to take 'em up.

My grandmother consoled me. "Don't worry, Q-tip—I mean Grandson—Ma'll take care of everything. It'll be okay." Ma could sew. You shoulda seen me our first game. I was the only guy on the floor with pleats in his pants! I hated basketball.

At last my big moment came. Huge game against our arch rival. So what it's only the "B" game before the varsity plays! Wasn't Sharon cheering? What else mattered? Game tied. Waning seconds. Coach outta players. Puts me in, pleats and all. God answers prayer: My shorts stay up, and my shot goes in! We beat North Pike! I'm a hero! Guess who runs out on the court to walk me off? You guessed it! Sharon Rogers!

Highlight of my life. "Don't trip. Watch those lines. Don't fall. Please voice, don't break. Sniff test. Do I need deodorant? Look cool. Oh no, here she is." "Hey," she says to me (my butter melts), "Do you know you're so skinny that when you shoot, we can count your ribs?"

Alas, so much for first loves. Since those days I've fallen in love with another who gives love freely. Unlike Sharon, this one knows I exist. Knows me. Loves me. Totally. Doesn't even count my skinny ribs but gave his skin and ribs for me. Guess it doesn't really matter that Sharon never knew me. But I can't help but hope she knows the one whose love we can all share-and share-alike.

> *Who will separate us from the love of Christ? . . .*
> *{nothing} will be able to separate us from the love of*
> *God in Christ Jesus our Lord. (Romans 8:35, 39)*

Of Floods, Falls, and Fathers

Flash flooding in northwest Arkansas resulted in millions of dollars in damage and at least one horror story, authorities said, as torrential rains pushed rivers over their banks.

Young Derek Perkins, age two of Rogers, Arkansas, fell from War Eagle Bridge into the raging, swollen waters of War Eagle Creek, reported Tom Jopling, paramedic for the Springdale fire department, who helped rescue the child.

The boy's father, Kenneth Perkins, jumped into the dark waters to save his son, who was completely submerged on at least two different occasions, according to bystanders. Mr. Perkins managed to retrieve his son, swim to a tree, and hang on for more than an hour while waiting for help.

The boy was reported to be in critical condition at Springdale Memorial Hospital after suffering from extreme hypothermia. "The boy was unresponsive to any painful stimulus at all," Jopling said. "His body was beginning to shut down." A spokesman for the hospital reported: "The boy is better, crying a bit, though still in need of care."

Why young humans are forever falling like this, I do not know. Why middle-aged humans forever fall and older humans fall, neither do I know. Why Derek fell, why Adam fell, why Eve fell, why I fell, I do not know. But why Kenneth Perkins jumped in after his son, I think I do understand. Had it been my young son Christopher who plunged headlong into the waters of death, could I have stood passively by and watched from above? Neither could our Father in heaven.

One day young Derek Perkins will hear the story of how his dad jumped into angry waters at War Eagle Creek to save him. It will move him. It will change him. How do I know so much? 'Cause God in Christ jumped in one day for Randall.

But God proves his love for us in that while we still were sinners Christ died for us. (Romans 5:8)

Name That Tune

The death of a 77-year-old miser with no known relatives or friends brought a horde of would-be heirs to the Ingham County probate court in Lansing, Michigan. Authorities said that after his death, at least 400 persons claimed blood ties to Henry Drummond.

Mr. Drummond, who died of natural causes in his $49-a-week room at the downtown YMCA, left behind $240,000 in nine banks from Denver to Boston, plus extensive holdings in stocks and bonds.

Paul Rosenbaum, the state-appointed attorney who handled Drummond's estate, said that hundreds of people asked "for checks who say they are second cousins twice-removed. It's like 'Send me a check; we'll figure out how I'm related later,'" he added.

Okay. Name that tune. Where have we heard that one before? Sung by a popular group known as "We Fickle Humans," it is called "I've got nothing for you, Hun, unless you've got something for me." The flip side? "Baby, I love you, but what's in it for me?"

In the book of Job, Satan, who seems to have human nature pretty well sized up, asks God cynically: "Does Job love God for nothing?" In other words, he scoffs, "Does Job love you for who you are God, or for what he can get out of it?

Seems some 400 would-be "friends and relatives" of a 77-year-old child of God rushed forward to answer Satan's question. And sadly enough, in incriminating fashion. This time, in relation to a neighbor.

But what about you? How must God answer Satan for you? And, for me? Are our relations with God and neighbor pure? Or are we "in it for what we can get out of it"?

I still love Billy Joel's song! Care to sing? "I love you just the way you are."

Beloved, let us love one another, because love is from God. (1 John 4:7a)

The Power of Love

You may know about the Foster Grandparent Program. This venture seeks to bring together children with high needs with foster grandparent volunteers who have love and time to give. Abused children, children with learning disorders, handicapped youngsters, or neglected little ones receive love, love, and more love from their surrogate grandparents. They also receive help and encouragement with schoolwork and life in general. These caring senior adults in return receive love and satisfaction from knowing their lives count as they bless little ones immeasurably.

Some stories are heartwarming; others rip your heart out. Child abuse, for instance, can be difficult to prove. Suspicion does not constitute a case. Evidence must be strong. Unfortunately, suspicion was present, but evidence was not in this particular Texas case. Officials could not yet help the little child.

Then it happened. One night the small child, battered, bloodied, tortured, was rushed by ambulance to the local emergency room. Screaming hysterically, she fought the doctors' and nurses' attempts to treat and dress her wounds. Like a rabid animal she raged, lashing out against any who dared draw near. With no other recourse, the nurses, themselves crying, forcefully held the young girl down on the table. As she screamed, struggling to break free, the doctors, working quickly, finished their sutures. Immediately, the child tore free. Crying madly, she dashed across the room. Curling up in a corner, assuming a fetal position, she wailed, letting no one come near.

One of the nurses called for the child's foster grandmother. When she arrived, the grandmother asked that a rocking chair from the nursery be brought down to the room. She then asked everyone to leave, leaving her alone with the hysterical little girl.

Rocking in the chair, she began to sing. "Jesus loves me this I know." Into the night she sang. "For the Bible tells me so." For 10 hours she sang. "Little ones to him belong. They are weak, but he is strong." 'Til dawn she sang. "Yes, Jesus loves me. Yes, Jesus loves me. Yes, Jesus loves me. The Bible tells me so."

When the doctors and nurses came into the room at dawn, they found the foster grandmother in the rocking chair, still rocking, still singing. And in her arms . . . was the little child.

> . . . *Let the little children come to me. (Matthew 19:14a)*

🐝 🐝 🐝

Fat Fullbacks and Aging Beauty Queens

Riding down Highway 65 south. Eudora, Arkansas. Tallulah, Louisiana. East on I-20. Vicksburg, Mississippi. Highway 27 south. Pine trees. Utica. Crystal Springs. I-55 south. Going home. McComb. Memories. Nostalgia. '60s music playing on the car stereo. Lennon and McCartney croon:

> *There are places I remember all my life,*
> *though some have changed.*
> *Some forever not for better,*
> *some have gone and some remain.*
> *All these places have their moments,*
> *with lovers and friends I still can recall.*
> *Some are dead, and some are living.*
> *In my life I've loved them all.*

Arrive home. Drive by the old school. Doors open. Turn around. Gotta go in. Revisit old ghosts. Reminisce. Don. Chuck. Barry. Dwight. Mary Emma. Dennis. Coach. Patsy. Gary. Randy.

Down the hall. On a ladder. Painting. Late. Surprise. "Need help? Remember me?" "Don't know if a brush'd fit your hand," the figure replies. "Been 20 years, Son. I remember you. What brings you back? Good to see you."

Later. Much. Catching up done. 20 years worth. Fun. Therapy. Laughter. What ifs. Could've beens. Magic moments. Versus North Pike. South Pike. Ups. Downs. Triumphs. Defeats. Updates. "Dwight's coaching. Barry made a preacher. Don't know whatever happened to Louis. Gary's still around. You sure could shoot a basketball. Skinniest calves in school. Glenn died a few years ago. So did Clifton. Killed in a car wreck. Patsy married, stayed around. Worked several jobs. Divorced. Moved. Eddie's a minister. Texas, I believe. Yeah, gettin' ready for inspection. Just gonna paint here a little longer."

"Assistant principal now, ya know. Comes with the turf." "Coach. Gotta be going. You look the same. Look great. Congratulations on making assistant principal. You deserve it. Tell the gang 'hi' for me. If any pass through, catch you on the ladder." "You take care, Son. I'll tell your ol' fullback buddy and homecoming queen 'hello' for ya. Last time I saw 'em one's kinda fat, other's fadin'."

Headlights beaming toward Little Rock. Late. Kay and girls sleep sweetly. I give thanks for past and present, especially present. Lennon-McCartney harmonize softly the last of their nostalgic ode:

> But of all these friends and lovers,
> There is no one compares with you
> and these memories lose their meaning,
> When I think of love as something new.
> Though I know I'll never lose affection,
> for people and things that went before.
> I know I'll often stop and think about them.
> In my life I love you more.
> In my life I love you more.

Who would've thought it? A left-right combination from Bible and Beatles? And straight to the heart:

Let your fountain be blessed, and rejoice in the wife of your youth, a lovely hind, a graceful doe. Let her affection fill you at all times with delight, be infatuated always with her love. (Proverbs 5:18-19, RSV)

38

Ma's Thanksgiving Table

We didn't have far to go to get to Grandma's house. Why we didn't go more than we did, I never figured out. Everybody was so happy there. Ma's Thanksgiving Table symbolized gospel for me long before I knew what gospel was.

There 'round danced merriment, love, laughter, oneness, food, warmth. It was all there. And people I loved: Mother and Daddy. Sue and Faye. Unca Buddy, Aunt Avis, Deryl, and Angie. Unca Gordon, Aunt Billy Faye, Gerry, Barry, and Candy. Billy Boy was born later. 'Course I was there. You couldn't of pulled me away with Pa's ol' mule. In heaven—that's where I was. Then there was Ma and Pa. Ma was heavy. Pa was tall.

Funny how everybody was something. Mother was from the country. Daddy worked for the newspaper and drove the new car. Sue was Suzy Q or Donna Sue Poo Poo. Named after her daddy (Donald), but she had Aunt Avis' blonde hair, everyone said. Faye was Mary Faye or just Mary or Mary, Mary Quite Contrary, the quiet little cherub.

Unca Buddy loved "to pick." He came to have fun. Unc would almost rather tease than eat. I said almost. Aunt Avis was the family belle: young, blonde, pretty, prissy, Unca Buddy's trophy. Deryl inherited his "apple of Ma's eye" status from Aunt Avis. He was the youngest grandson: little tough guy, good athlete, "Bubby" to Angie. Angie, the youngest granddaughter, was sweet, as angelic as her name, Hula-Hoop champ.

Unca Gordon, the ex-Marine, asked no quarter, took none, ran his family like a boot camp. He said "Frog"; I said "Dribbett." Aunt Billy Faye was wise and warm, had loving eyes. Gerry, the quarterback sensation, was the oldest. Barry put up with Gerry. Barry had a great laugh: fun guy, my age, one month older, good athlete, Injun fighter. Candy didn't like boys—forever.

We all had our own identity. And it weren't no use buckin' the peckin' order neither, 'cause it had been established before the foundation of the world.

Ah, Thanksgiving memories. We've all grown up, married, have children of our own now. Parents then, are grandparents now. Of course, the magic of the season lives on. And on, and on . . .

This Thanksgiving I'm thankful, thankful for family, thankful to be a part of God's family, and thankful to be going back home—where for me, "The gospel first became flesh." May your thanksgiving be as filling.

And men shall come from east and west, and from north and south, and sit at table in the kingdom of God. (Luke 13:29, RSV)

🐝 🐝 🐝

Pa Used To Cook on a Boat

My grandmother and grandfather O'Brien were "Ma" and "Pa" to us kids. That's what we called 'em, 'cause that's who they were—just Ma and Pa. Ma could cook. Now most all of the womenfolk in Pike County, Mississippi, can cook. But Ma, she could really cook! Some of my fondest childhood memories seat me at Ma's table at Thanksgiving with family: the O'Briens, the Dickersons, the Millers. Good kin and good cooking's hard to beat.

Guess my favorite mealtime at Ma and Pa's, though, was suppertime. Suppertime was when Pa would cook. There was something wonderful about watching those giant hands breaking those little eggs, stirring those grits, flipping that sizzlin' bacon, cooking "breakfast for supper." Gosh, I loved being with Pa! Just me and Pa in the kitchen. Well, just me and Pa and a few stories, that is.

"Pa, how'd you learn to cook so good?" I'd ask. Pa would sniff his nose like he didn't wanna brag and say, "I used to cook on a boat." "Wow, a boat, Pa? Did you really cook on a boat?" I'd ask in awe, visions of Tom Sawyer dancing in my head. "Yeah, back a long time ago I did. I cooked on a boat."

"Pa, why'd you tell that boy you cooked on a boat? You ain't never cooked on no boat!" Ma scolded, as she overheard Pa braggin' and rushed into the kitchen to take charge. "Helen, I did too cook on a boat!" Pa insisted. "That was before you knew me." "Psh-shaw, Pa!" Ma would say. "You ain't cooked on no boat. Why you ain't never been on no boat." Then she turned to me and said, "Hun, your Pa ain't never cooked on no boat."

In *The Cocktail Party* by T. S. Elliot, one of the characters, who is slightly inebriated, leans over and whispers to a psychiatrist at the party: "Please make me feel important." Elliot is, of course, showing us ourselves. We all want to feel important, don't we?

So . . . did Pa ever really cook on a boat? Some of my kin down in Pike County Mississippi, think my Pa ain't never cooked on no boat, that he was just trying to look important to a little boy who worshiped him. Wanna know what I think? Pa used to cook on a boat. Wanna know what else I think? I think that, in Christ, we all used to cook on boats.

Knee-ology, Mother, and Me

Journey to McComb, Mississippi. Wind your way through the streets to Westview Circle, 238. Go in through the back door, announcing your arrival as you enter. "Back door guests are best," invites the brown sign on the wall by the door.

Walk through the kitchen. Signs everywhere. Ceramic. Magnetic. Wooden. "Irene's Kitchen." "Kiss the Cook." And on the fridge, "Calories Ahead."

Make your way into the den. Irene and Donald O'Brien's den. Cozy. Warm. Feel it. Enjoy the fellowship. Relax. "Ewes ain't fat; ewes is fluffy," teases the sign. Stitchings. Sayings. Everywhere. "If your day is hemmed with prayer, it is less likely to unravel." "Give thanks unto the Lord." "When God closes a door, He opens a window."

Folksy sayings all. But you're reading theology from my favorite homespun theologian: Mother. Her humble knee-ology (prayer, love, and more prayer) exceeds my loftiest grasps at theology. Her folksy theology, available in ceramic or needlepoint, translates easily but profoundly

"Back door guests are best."—Hospitality
"Ewes ain't fat; ewes is fluffy."— Acceptance
"When God closes a door, He opens a window."—Trust

Read the rest, and you'll find prayer, love, thanksgiving, praise, and more. Not bad stuff for those who would follow Christ.

Please forgive me for the public airing of my private ruminations. Guess returning home for Mother's open-heart surgery nostalgically reminds me of my wonderful debt to her. How thankful I am! I've been born twice. And she's responsible for both.

Her children rise up and call her happy. (Proverbs 31:28a)

SIN

Sold Again

Little Rock police reported that a 14' bronze crucifix that had stood at the entrance to the city's Calvary Cemetery for more than half a century was stolen sometime between December 9 and 14, 1988. Thieves apparently backed a large truck up to the crucifix, tied a rope around it, and broke it off at the base.

Irene Bell, cemetery manager, reported the value of the crucifix at $50,000 or five times its original value of $10,000 when donated in 1930 by the late Catholic bishop John B. Morriss. The cemetery offered a $1,000 reward for return of the cross, no questions asked.

Authorities said, however, that all that remained of the stolen crucifix was a fragment bearing the inscription *INRI*, translated "Jesus of Nazareth, King of the Jews." The fragment was found at Rixey Iron and Metal Company, a North Little Rock salvage yard, where scrap metal goes for 50 cents a pound. Apparently the cross had been cut into small pieces before being sold. Ironically, the 900-pound cross brought only $450.00, less than half the reward offered.

Poor thieves (two were arrested). Like Judas who sold Christ for 30 pieces of silver, sending the Saviour's broken body to a salvage yard named Golgotha, the thieves chose riches over righteousness, and lost both. In seeking to grow rich, they became poor. "I just feel like the person or persons who stole it won't have much peace for the rest of their lives," Bell lamented.

How tragic. We who could have riches in heaven are forever tempted to choose a few dollars on earth instead. Golgothas, junkyards, thirty pieces of silver here, a few hundred dollars there, the Christ, a cross, you, and me—all part of the grand cosmic drama. And once again, Christ is sold for less than the reward available. What are we doing to ourselves?

[Judas] said, "What will you give me if I betray him to you?" They paid him thirty pieces of silver. (Matthew 26:15)

Unca Buddy and Sputnik

Unca Buddy loved practical jokes. Next to impractical jokes, they were his favorite kind. Long as he could get your goat, Unca Buddy was happy—'less you had two goats.

Sputnik, named after the Soviet satellite, was our dog. Meaner 'n Kruschev's mother-in-law, Sputnik launched humans. Chewed Achilles' tendons. Knawed ankle bones. Unzipped calf muscles. We're talkin' K-9 plasma junkie here. Fangs like drinking straws, the predator bit everything that moved—'cept family. Woulda bit us too, but we offered to sleep under the steps. Gave him the house.

Once Unca Buddy came across the ugliest Halloween mask he'd ever seen. Now, Mother is deathly afraid of haints. Unca Buddy, o' course, made it his bidness to know such things. Come Halloween, dark falls. Onto our front porch lurks evil-looking, devilish Unca Buddy. Mother opens the door. The spook lunges! Screamin', nearly faintin', mother heareth the laughter not. Recoverin', she screams again. All Unca Buddy remembers hearing? "Sic him, Sputnik!"

If ever you should find yourself in Port Gibson, Mississippi, look up police chief Buddy Miller, won't ya? Tell him his Baptist preacher nephew would like him to comment on his ol' friend Sputnik. . . . From your jail cell, remember never to listen to me again. Sorry. "Like uncle, like nephew." Guess we all could stand to remember: Life is the pits when . . . you dig them for others.

Whoever digs a pit will fall into it. (Ecclesiastes 10:8a)

Away in a Manger

Our family had Baby Jesus right where we wanted him. Right where he's supposed to be, you'd think, this Christmas and all Christmases. Strategically, indeed celestially, placed in the center of our Holy Land-carved, Bethlehem-purchased, genuine olive wood nativity scene lies Baby Jesus. Asleep on the hay where he belongs, right?

Well, Baby Jesus keeps turning up missing. Suspect Christopher, who doesn't understand. He thinks it's okay to take Little Lord Jesus out of the manger. He thinks it's okay to move him around the house. Well, it's not.

One morning Little Lord Jesus appears in the bathroom. Start of a busy day, a hectic day. Three of us arguing strongly over who had the mirror first. I see him first. Then the others. Quiet falls. Then all: "Christopher! What is Lord Jesus doing in our bathroom?"

Comes Sunday. Christopher insists on taking Little Lord Jesus to church. We argue with him. He insists. I try. "Here is a candy cane, darling. Give Daddy Baby Jesus." No dice. Kay tries. "There's too much going on at church, Chris. Baby Jesus will get lost." Quiet.

"All is quiet. All is calm?" Not necessarily. Baby Jesus turns up this Christmas in our bedrooms, at the table for our evening meals, and even in the worst of all possible places. Can you believe this one? The other day here we are all piled headlong into the family car—all five of us—waging words, discussing in family terms (all against all) who knows what. When, you guess it, there staring up at us is Little Lord Jesus. In the family car, for goodness sakes! Is no place sacred?

Christopher just doesn't understand. But isn't that just like a child? To innocently love and want to carry with him that which he loves? How sweet. Oh well, we were all little children once, weren't we? For those of us who are older and wiser now, however, we can see to it that Baby Jesus stays right where he belongs this Christmas season . . . safely, quietly, . . . away in a manger.

A little child shall lead them. (Isaiah 11:6c)

Pride Goeth before the Alarm

On March 27, 1987, an honor bigger than my head came my way. Not to worry. My readily adjustable head size inflates as occasion demands. Or should I say over-inflates?

On Friday morning at 9:30 o'clock, the worship of God in Marquand Chapel, Yale Divinity School, was to occur. Yours truly, most humble servant of the Living God, had been invited to participate as a worship leader. I do not know if anyone else was impressed with me, but I was.

This was Marquand Chapel, Yale University. Home of the prestigious Beecher Lectures, where some of Christendom's most distinguished ministers had preached or lectured. Heady wine, indeed, for this simple redneck south Mississippi country boy.

Friday morning came. I showed up punch drunk on self-importance, staggering with my six-pack of pride, ego, insecurity, self-delusion, blindness, and stupidity. Worshiping God was a theoretical impossibility. I was worshiping me.

The service began. As I read Scripture pompously, the alarm on my watch sounded. My moment in the hallowed spotlight, mind you! And my alarm went off! I tried to turn it off. Nothing doing. I clutched the watch to muffle it. Didn't work. Everyone heard it. Looking now. Major disruption. Let's sing. During the hymn I shoved the nuisance under a pew cushion. The alarm continued. Clearly malfunctioning. Why me?

During the sacred, silent rite of communion, while reverently presiding at the Lord's table, what did my ears hear? What did all our ears hear? That watch! Beeping in prophetic protest from beneath the cushion! Ruining Randall's reverent religious ritual. Did it ever stop? Oh yes . . . when I did.

I will put an end to the pride of the arrogant. (Isaiah 13:11b)

🐝 🐝 🐝

Out Came This Calf

You don't have to tell me, unless you want to. I already know. Moses, right? Of the two brothers, you relate to Moses. Out of the fire speaks God to Moses. Out of the fire leaps god to Aaron. God's man, god's man. "Moses, this is God." "Cow, this is Aaron."

Well, I'm confessing. The one worshiping the golden calf is me. Remember the story? See Moses spend time alone with God on the holy mountain. See Moses receive the Ten Commandments. See Aaron fashion a golden calf with matching designer altar. See Aaron be a fool.

College will save me; make me somebody. . . . Cow, this is Randall. Athletics will take me to the Promised Land. . . . Captain Calf, Captain O'Brien; Captain O'Brien, Captain Calf. Seminary, master's degree, doctorate . . . Prominence, salvation is on the way! Publish . . . or perish. Ivy League . . . Yale. Books . . . author. These are your gods, O Israel. . . .

Woe is me. When will we ever learn? Our golden calves always do the only thing golden calves can ever do: fail us! A week, two, a month, two, and the thrill is gone. Then, alas, I need saving all over again. Eventually we all get caught worshiping idols, don't we? Career, significant other, a dream —would-be saviors all!

Tragedy of tragedies, like Israel's jewelry, a lot of precious things, sometimes persons, get thrown into the fire, sacrificed to our gods. Yet, like our brother Aaron, we refuse to accept our guilt. "I threw it into the fire, and out came this calf" (Exod 32:24).

What about you? Ever fashioned a golden calf? Worshiped one? Looked for meaning in some person, thing, dream, or event other than God? If, like me, you can relate to our brother Aaron, why not consider as a model his ultimate response? With the threat of death to sinners imminent, Moses demanded, "Who is on the Lord's side?" Aaron cold-cocked the calf. Have you?

You shall have no other gods before me. (Exodus 20:3)

The Fall of Humankind

Roch Pierre Charmet, the most prolific parachutist in history, plunged to his death Monday, February 20, 1989, when his parachute failed to open properly. The 59-year-old Frenchman, whose name appears in the *Guinness Book of World Records*, died, a veteran of 14,000 jumps.

Authorities said that Charmet folded his own chute. Truth is, it seems to me, we all do. In life as in skydiving, I, and none other, am responsible, ultimately, for Randall ... for choices, for carelessness, for consequences.

We pack our own chutes. The stakes are high. In skydiving, faulty folds force fatal falls. So, too, in life. Careless choices cause certain consequences. Ask Adam, or Eve.

What about you? Spiritually, have you grown careless? You might wanna check. The fold of the chute, it appears, still decides the fall of humankind. Look before you leap.

. . . Choose this day whom you will serve, . . . but as for me and my household, we will serve the Lord. (Joshua 24:15)

🐝 🐝 🐝

"Foul Shot"?

In hoops, a.k.a. roundball, basketball, etc., you have the hook shot, set shot, and jump shot. There is the dunk shot, the two-point shot, the three-point shot, the bank shot. But Larry McPherson, age 23, of 517 East 20th Street, Little Rock, Arkansas, gives new meaning to the term "foul shot."

McPherson was convicted April 7 of first-degree battery in the shooting of another Little Rock man over an alleged bad call in a basketball game. Seems McPherson intervened in a heated argument between two other players over a foul called near the end of a close game. Authorities said that McPherson walked off the court, pulled a gun from a bag under a tree, and fired several shots at James Simpson, the opposing player who disputed the call. Simpson, age 30, was hit once in the left leg and once in the groin, according to deputy prosecuting attorney Chris Tarver. During the trial, circuit judge Floyd Lofton asked McPherson why he had shot Simpson. McPherson said it was to be expected in close games.

Ahhh, the ol' foul shot! Somehow methinks this is not what James Naismith had in mind. McPherson's novel interpretation of the rules could conceivably lend new meaning to the phrase "The Final Four." And what about fan excitement!? Highlights of hockey . . . begone! Give us a foul shot!

Well, time to draw my moral from all this: First, "Fools show their anger at once" (Prov 12:16). Next, Baptist deacons meetings now fall into second place for "most violent game in town." Last, dear reader (sorry, lessons of redeeming value are hard to find in this story), please pray for Simpson's rebound. And, please, whatever you do, don't get in any close basketball games with Larry McPherson. I hear the man shoots a mean foul shot.

Folly is the garland of fools. (Proverbs 14:24b)

Pride Goeth before a Title

Have you noticed how many of us preacher types insist on being called "Doctor" these days? And how almost every self-respecting church seems to demand a "doctor" in the pulpit? Many of us "doctors" have never attended seminary, and some of us have not finished college. Yet, we have our "doctorates."

Don't ask me why. Maybe we are trying to mask our deeply-rooted inferiority feelings, both pastor and church. Perhaps the title is a badge telling the world we are okay, when we ourselves are not quite convinced. Who knows?

A friend in the ministry calls me (or has his secretary call and put me on hold) and identifies himself as "Dr. So-and-so." Even his wife speaks of her husband in the third person, with title. Bless their hearts. They bought their degree through the mail. They are not alone. Countless ministers do the same.

Of course, many of us with earned doctorates are equally arrogant. Sometimes, we write diatribes denouncing titles. Reverse elitism, we might call it. Truth is, we're all just prideful sinners—all of us. Seems we all worry more about self than service.

As Richard Foster points out, however, Christ chose towel over title. Can't you just hear Christ now? "Now

Simon Peter, let Dr. Jesus take a look at that toe-jam." Pride goeth before a title; humility goeth before a towel.

Signed,
The Really Right Reverend Doctor Randall

. . . I say to everyone among you not to think of yourself more highly than you ought to think. (Romans 12:3a)

Lite Church

Maybe it had to happen. I dunno. In this age of lite beer, lite mayonnaise, and lite syrup, I suppose it's no wonder we now have—are you ready for this—lite church.

Surprised? Should you be? After all, haven't we moderns enjoyed lite commitment for years now? Haven't lite vows been the rage for well over a decade? (Witness our divorce rate). Apparently, the commercial we're not hearing is that lite love is one-third less fulfilling.

Anyway, the current trend is clear. There is lite Miracle Whip, lite beer, lite bread, and now lite church—all less filling. Have you seen the ad?

Lite Church

43% less visitation
24% fewer commitments
39% fewer tithers (home of the 5% tithe)
51% fewer baptisms and decisions at invitation
44% fewer commitments to happy marriages and home
Only 7 commandments—your choice
Tastes Great!
Everything you always wanted in a church . . . and less!

Spiritual Bankruptcy

Traveling to and from work each day I pass by a building that is a deep curiosity to me. Something is manufactured on site, yet the front of the facility resembles a modern office complex, with its beautiful mirrored glass and sophisticated appearance. Only from the sides of the complex can one tell that this is a factory and not a suite of professional offices.

Yet the elegance of this striking edifice is marred. In the place of the lovely mirrored glass in the front of this designer masterpiece, at three separate locations, stand three very ugly sheets of plywood. Ill repair over the years has, regrettably, resulted in a snaggle-tooth look to this otherwise stunning architectural face.

Recently, I noticed that the plant had closed. Operations ceased altogether. Care to guess what this failed business once produced? You won't believe it. Enhanced Glass. That's the company's name, or was. No wonder their façade was so magnificently different from other factories. So beautiful . . . once.

Alas, years passed. In time the company no longer used its own product, though it continued to sell to others. First stage: Others noticed, business suffered. Second stage: Doors closed, out-of-business, town talk. Final stage: Regrettable? Shame really. Don't you think?

The other day while driving by, shaking my head at the sad folks at Enhanced Glass, a sudden sinking feeling came over me. "And what about you, Reverend O'Brien? Do you still use the product you sell?" "Who me?" I said. "Or the church?" "Either?" came the voice. "Either."

For the shepherds have become stupid, and have not sought the Lord; therefore they have not prospered . . .
(Jeremiah 10:21, NASB)

Shades of Maeyken Wens?

Maeyken Wens, an Anabaptist sister of years gone by, was arrested for proclaiming the gospel of Jesus Christ as she understood it from her personal reading of Scripture. Imprisoned and tortured for six months, she was forced to repent and recant. When she would not, she was sentenced to death, October 5, 1573. Included in her sentence read by the court was instruction that her tongue be screwed fast to the roof of her mouth so that she might not preach Jesus along the way to the place of burning.

The next day her teenage son, Adriaen, took his youngest brother, three-year-old Hans Matthews, so that her first and last born might be present at her death. When the execution began, Adriaen fainted and missed his mother's parting. But when it was over, Adriaen and Hans sifted through the simmering ashes to find and to clutch the screw with which their mother's tongue had been stilled.

Exit 1573. Enter 1987. Did you see where Prescott Memorial Baptist Church in Memphis prayed for one year in seeking a minister for the congregation? They called Nancy H. Sehested, the daughter and granddaughter of Southern Baptist ministers. And did you see where the 400 male messengers of the Shelby Baptist Association quickly moved to censure Reverend Sehested and the church by expelling the congregation?

The Lord reminds us, "In the last days, . . . I will pour out my Spirit upon all flesh, and your sons and your daughters shall prophesy. . . . Even upon my slaves, both men and women, in those days I will pour out my Spirit; and they shall prophesy" (Acts 2:17, 18). If this is so, then for what reason do we, the children of Maeyken Wens, and the children of her children, lift up the corkscrew used against our maternal ancestor? To inspire? . . . Or . . . To threaten?

McMessage

Remember when churches held protracted meetings, revivals lasting two and three weeks? Remember when preachers would preach for hours (watch it!), and communities loved it? Remember the white picket fences and paperboys on bicycles? Neighborhood churches? And supper, fresh from the fields? When the still small voice within was called conscience, not Sony Walkman?

Okay, I admit it. Yes, I loved the Saturday Evening Post, Norman Rockwell, and the Country Parson. Sawdust trails gave birth to a lot of us back then. Those long hot summer night sermons underneath that open-air tabernacle (ruggedly built with 12-inch poles, tin roof, and straightback wooden pews) caused us to get saved enough times, one of 'em had to take.

Well, goodbye Norman. Hello 1990s, the age of drive-thru worship. Can I get that hymn to go please?" "Welcome to the Church of the Golden Arches!" Sermons? McNuggets or "Mac, muff it!" And you? What do you think of these new-fangled trends?

Seems to me something is lost when white picket fences and friendly collies give way to burglar bars and pit bulls. When country cookin', in the kitchen or the pulpit, loses out to fast food. Then again, who knows? Maybe I'm just a bit old-fashioned. Still, in a rapidly changing world of "lite sin," it's just hard to believe that what we really need on Sunday is a good ol' McMessage.

Humpty Dumpty Goes to Church

Humpty Dumpty sat on the wall.
Humpty Dumpty had a great fall.
All the king's horses and all the king's men
Couldn't put Humpty Dumpty together again.

Remember this doggerel? And remember our lesson? From Monsieur Egg we first learned that sitting on walls is dangerous. Translated: Life is risky business, threatening, fragile. So we learned to be careful, sober, sane. Remember?

Not much new here. Senōr Egg has a knack for falling. But wait! Woe is me. Don't we all have a knack for falling? Ever since the original fall of humankind (Gen 3), seems we good eggs have been tottering on walls of our own. Lovingly, however, a steadying hand comes to us from God.

Apparently, our new lesson is this: We can either be steadied by God's Word or, like our old friend Humpty, be an egg, over easy.

Now to him who is able to keep you from falling . . . be glory . . . (Jude 24-25)

That Was the Last Time I Went Duck Hunting

Do I remember it? As if I could ever forget it! It's January of '84. Ray Baxter, Gary Arnold, and I are holed up in some dingy duck hunter's "motel" in DeWitt, Arkansas. Baxter, Benton's proud answer to Mutual of Omaha's Marlin Perkins, had insisted that his fellow lawyer, Arnold, and interim pastor, yours truly, join him in brave and patriotic pursuit of that deadly terror to our women and children, the Stuttgart duck.

"God bless America as we fight to keep our windshields clean," Baxter croons as he turns out the light and hits the hay. Arnold and I, by necessity, are sharing a bed—a small bed, a very small bed—awkwardly, like hanging off the side so as not to touch legs in the middle and stuff.

Fast forward the tape. Stop. Push play. See Randall awaking before dawn. See Randall's eyes become the size of

Hula-Hoops. See him eat his pillow to muffle the scream. "Yikes!! How to get out of this without waking Arnold! Can you believe this? How long has my leg been over him like this? What if he wakes up? I'm ruined! Got to be very careful here. Easy does it, nice and easy." Slowly, I lift my leg. Ever so slowly . . . gradually I lift my . . . "Good morning Preacher." Uh-oh . . .

What about you? Ever found yourself in a situation that shamed you? Ever been caught having to explain something you couldn't? Accidental anguish or intentional iniquity, don't you hate the humiliation? Not Judah. Jeremiah accused Judah of "sinning without shame," of being "too bad to blush." Judgment was certain.

Good news! God relieves the pain of the penitent. To put it another way: "Blessed are the blushers, for they shall not be called blockheads." Thank heavens for forgiveness. But as far as duck hunting goes, Lord, this blessed blusher shall be called retired.

> *. . . They committed abomination; yet they were not ashamed, they did not know how to blush. (Jeremiah 6:15)*

DEATH

Quiet Desperation

Most men live their lives in quiet desperation.

—Thoreau

Something horrible happened this week, and I don't feel so good. I can only conclude that I didn't have the same effect upon him that he had upon me. I recall his smile, corny attempts at wit, pleasant greetings to Kay or the girls (if they beat me to the mail), sincere reverence for my calling as he greeted me without fail as "Reverend." . . . "Nice day, Reverend." . . . Always Reverend.

How many days over the past couple of years did he find tired spirits and sagging shoulders at the end of my driveway —at the end of my day—only to leave "Reverend" smiling again, spirits buoyed, steps quickened on the short walk to the family door, mail securely in hand?

Were Jeremiah's lamentations reborn daily, witnessed by my blind eyes? "Is it nothing to all you who pass by? Look and see if there is any pain like my pain" (Lam 1:12).

So many questions I never asked. So many words I never spoke. So many opportunities I never took. So many touches we never touched. "Man is a subject in quest of a predicate," wrote Herschel.

This week he, a 28-year-old mailman, husband of only two years, and a friend of mine (who never heard me say it nor seldom saw me show it) chose his macabre predicate: death—suicide.

Some Reverend! . . . didn't even know his name. . . . As I confessed, I don't feel so good.

I Miss Floyd

December 29, 1995, 9:32 AM. My phone rings. "Hello Randall, this is Van. I have some bad news. It's about Floyd. He's dead. Hung himself in the church." "WHAT!" "The maid found him this morning when she came in, 7:45." "No! Oh No! Oh God, no!" Just like that I learn my friend of 20 years is dead. . . . Shock, searing pain, howls, tears . . . "Oh God, no!"

Drove to Kentwood, Louisiana (population 2,000), where Floyd spent some of his childhood years. His dad once owned an automobile dealership there. Got a haircut where Floyd got his hair cut as a boy. Bought a suit of clothes for the funeral at Simmons Men's Store on Main Street where Floyd shopped as a little boy. Reflected. Talked to Mr. Russell Bridges. Listened to Mr. Russell Bridges. Listened some more. Resident sage. 70 years old. Bachelor. "Randall," he said, "let me tell you about Charlie Lindsey." "Sure," I said. So he began.

"Charlie's dead now. Died a few years back. Old. Broken. Tired. Drunk mostly. Every day of Charlie's life he bought a newspaper. First thing, every morning. Carried it in his back pocket all day long. Had a nice pen and pencil set he carried in his front shirt pocket. Everywhere he went he carried that newspaper and pen and pencil set. But Randall, Charlie Lindsey couldn't read or write. First thing every morning, long as I can remember, from the time he was a young man 'til the time he died, Charlie Lindsey carried that newspaper in his backpocket and that pen and pencil set in his front pocket. But Charlie Lindsey couldn't read or write a word."

I caught on. My friend Floyd was a minister whose own pain was camouflaged by his ministering to the pain of others. But the story of Charlie Lindsey is bigger than that. I mean, is that us or what? We're all Charlie Lindsey! To what extreme do we go to hide our pain? To what extent do we go to conceal our inadequacies, our hurts, our needs? And, God forbid, just where does that road lead? . . . I miss Floyd.

Come to me, all you that are weary and are carrying heavy burdens, and I will give you rest. (Matthew 11:28)

🐝 🐝 🐝

Lennon, Maravich, and Me

One drew unprecedented crowds with his music; the other with his magic. Yet both were musical, both magical, each larger than life, pied pipers two.

We dreamed of playing guitar like one, of shooting basketball like the other. Beatles and basketball: that's who we were back then—John Lennon and Pistol Pete. Models they were, icons, islands in the storm-tossed seas of the '60s.

And now they are both gone. First John, then Pete. Along with JFK, RFK, and Martin. All dead, all murdered. Except the Pistol, who died of a heart attack while playing pickup basketball. He was only 40. "It seems the good die young." The song is right.

Lennon and the Beatles sold records; Maravich set them. He led the nation in scoring three straight years, and his career average of 44.2 points per game remains an NCAA record. He was also an inductee into the NBA Hall of Fame.

But Pete knew there was more to life than throwing rocks in a can. Searching for something, anything, he began to drink. He dabbled in astrology, astronomy, mysticism, and vegetarianism, becoming a nutrition freak. Next came UFOs and an obsession with the extraterrestrial. For almost 20 years he abused alcohol.

Then Pete Maravich accepted Jesus as Lord and Savior. The Pistol became a lay preacher, giving his testimony at basketball clinics and churches everywhere. He was a doting father and a devoted husband. At last, Pete had found peace.

Of all the magnificent moves Pistol Pete ever made, he felt his greatest was off the court: accepting Christ as his personal Lord. "I wouldn't trade my relationship with Jesus Christ for anything in all the world," he loved to relate.

Well, the '60s have gone the way of all flesh. And my teen years are, I'm afraid, as distant as the "Ed Sullivan Show." Anyway, we know now there's nothing eternal about either guitar or basketball. Yet, once again Pistol Pete is an inspiration to me. He was in California to lead a focus on the Christian family when he died.

The Bible says, "It is appointed once for every man to die." And then again, "Whoever calls upon the name of the Lord shall be saved." Pete's in heaven. I only hope that Lennon, Maravich, and me will one day be one, two, three.

How can we escape if we neglect so great a salvation? (Hebrews 2:3a)

Wanted: Dead or Alive?

The opposite of joy is not sorrow, but unbelief.
—Leslie Weatherhead

"We don't believe in God; we just say we do. God is dead!" Those were the words of theologians and philosophers in the early '60s. Even *Time* magazine (April 8, 1966) ran a cover story titled "Is God Dead?"

According to the alleged experts in these matters, the West has moved from theism to anti-theism to post-theism. Ours is now a post-Christian era, we are told.

Ironically, according to the Gallup polls, we are still highly religious, but God is dead. Our religiosity, our lack of real faith, has killed God. Modern man in a scientific age is finding that God is no longer necessary, or perhaps that God is neither necessary or unnecessary: God is simply irrelevant; God is dead.

In his book, *Called to Preach, Condemned to Survive*, Clayton Sullivan relates that Paul Pittman once compared the sentiment surrounding religion to an old grandfather's clock. The clock has been in the family for years, but doesn't work anymore. Sullivan says, "For nothing in the world would one get rid of Grandfather's clock. Indeed, it is polished and dusted regularly and has a place of honor in the living room. Yet no one expects Grandfather's clock to tell time or to regulate life."

What do you think? Is religion simply an heirloom of the human family? A nonfunctioning but revered antique? Is the church becoming the dinosaur of the 20th century? Is real Christianity dying out? Is God dead, as some insist?

We attend church each Sunday dressed "real pretty." We wear fine dresses and new suits. But are we dressed for God's funeral or for an encounter with the risen, living, Lord Jesus Christ? Truth is, only you can decide for which you have dressed.

He is . . . risen. (Luke 24:5b)

Ready or Not?

Nearly 25 years ago I wrote a simple humorous little song to use at youth fellowships. Hopefully entertaining, certainly unsophisticated, "The Basketball Song," as it became known, was one feeble attempt to package the theology of the cross in the dress of fun and sport. It went something like this:

The game was played on Sunday in heaven's own backyard.
Satan brought the basketball and two 6'10" guards.
The angels in the grandstand let out a great big yell.
Jesus hit a jump shot against the boys from hell.

(Chorus)
Go with God. Go with God.
Jesus hit it one more time.
Ol' Moses at guard, he's looking real fine.
Go with God. Go with God.
Rock 'em. Sock 'em. Jesus, pop 'em.
Go with God.

The game is fully underway; both teams fight to go forward.
Jesus jumping center and Moses playing guard,
The angels in the grandstand started throwing their paper cups
Moses doing the best he can just missed another layup.

(Chorus same as above except:)
Jesus hit it one more time.
Ol' Moses, big gunner, must be blind.

Trailing by one with seconds to play, a victory seems a myth.
But as the horn ends the game, Satan commits his fifth.
The angels in the grandstand let out a great big yell.
Jesus hit a one-and-one to beat the boys from hell.

(Chorus same except:)
Though my story is kinda tall,
There's a lesson here for you all.
Go with God. Go with God.
"Big G," little "od," go with God.

The careful student of junk jingles for Jesus, who has nothing better to do, will notice the metaphoric inferences in stanza 1 to our sin problem and the incarnation, the inadequacy of the law in stanza 2, in stanza 3 the apparent victory of Satan in Christ's crucifixion, and then finally the triumphant analogy of the resurrection.

Well, anyway, the song came back to me when Pistol Pete Maravich died. Somehow in that mysteriously platonic drama of redemption being played out on heaven's cosmic court, God now has a super team consisting of Moses, Jesus, 6'5" Maravich, and (since it's my idea, song, and book) 5'11" Randall O'Brien. (The last player is a future draft pick. Distant, I trust).

But that's only four—room for one more. Interested? The Pistol's surprise death reminds all of us: "You gotta be ready to play; you never know when your number may be called."

For everything there is a season, . . . a time to be born, and a time to die. (Ecclesiastes 3:1, 2a)

They're Playing Our Song

They're playing our song. Not that we like it. 'Cause we don't. Hate it, in fact. It's their song—not ours. Who cares what John Donne said? That bell ain't tolling for none of me. Hate that bell and its macabre song.

It's their song—not ours. Into the night they dance that eerie waltz with the Grim Reaper, Elvis, Belushi, Baez, Prom Night Boys . . . Drugs and death go steady. You know that.

Hey. Even King, Lennon, Kennedy, and Kennedy put their quarter in the jukebox. You don't tug on Superman's cape. And you don't mess around with truth in a world that hates it. But Maravich? 40. I give up. Why? Next Don Golden, 24, star of LSU's Final Four basketball team a few short years ago. Dead. Natural causes. Exit Andy Gibb, 30, of

Bee Gees fame. Gone. This is too much. Now Ron Brown, Secretary of Commerce. Who else?

"Now this bell tolling softly for another, says to me, 'Thou must die.'" Donne said that and more.

> When one man dies, one chapter is not torn out of the book, but translated into a better language; and every chapter must be so translated; God employs several translators; some pieces are translated by age, some by sickness, some by war, some by justice; but God's hand is in every translation.
>
> No man is an island, entire of itself; every man is a piece of the continent, a part of the main; if a clod be washed away by the sea, Europe is the less; ... any man's death diminishes me, because I am involved in mankind; and therefore never send to know for whom the bell tolls; it tolls for thee.

We hate it. I do. But woe is me. Their song is our song. Alas, the biological clock is ticking. "All flesh is grass," says the prophet. The bell tolls.

For what, or for whom, are you living? Methinks we'd better make life count—quick. Not that we like it. But I'm afraid they're playing our song.

... It is appointed for mortals to die once, and after that the judgment. (Hebrews 9:27)

QUEST

Journeying Together

Once there was a man who went for a walk in the forest and got lost. He wandered around for hours trying to find his way out of the dark woods. First in fear, then hope, then fear again, he wandered, trying one path after another. But none of them led out.

Suddenly the man came across another person strolling through the forest. He cried out, "Thank God for another human being! Can you show me the way back to town?" The other man replied, "No, I'm lost, too. But we can help each other in this way. We can tell each other which paths we have already tried and been disappointed in. That will help us find the one that leads out."

So goes it. The forest, so senseless, so intimidating when we traverse it alone, is never so hopeless in community. How good it feels to be a part of each other, to find hope in journeying together, to go in search of ultimate meaning . . . together.

How 'bout it? Shall we journey together? Is there one you would ask to join us? Why not do it? Who knows? We may even encounter the One who leads out of the forest.

Murka and You

Two years ago Murka, a gray and white cat, was banished from her home in Moscow for eating two canaries. For her sins Murka's owners exiled her to Voronezh, a village 400 miles away, or roughly the distance from Little Rock to New Orleans. Today she is home.

The feline's odyssey was recounted in the newspaper *Komsomolskaya Pravda* in November 1989, and subsequently reported by the Associated Press. Vladimir Dontsov,

Murka's owner, expelled the offending feline after the family's second pet canary was killed in less than a year. One year and 400 miles later, Dontsov spotted the cat coming home. Dirty, hungry, and missing part of her tail, Murka struggled home. Also she was pregnant.

Apparently, felines and humans have at least this much in common. We are not purr-fect. Were not Adam and Eve banished from the garden of Eden, in Murka-like fashion? Our sins do find us out—apples, canaries, you name it. But we do have cause for hope. The parable of the prodigal son promises much.

If our God cares enough about lost cats to create within our furry friends both the burning desire and the ability to find their way home, then surely God has placed within each of us, His children, no lesser desire or ability to "come home."

So how 'bout it, dear prodigal? Dirty? Hungry? Tired? Worse for the wear? You could come home. Murka or maiden, feline or fellow, wherever you are, your Master has put the candle in the window and the welcome mat out.

Let us test and examine our ways, and return to the Lord. (Lamentations 3:40)

On Seeing Chuck Again

Things ain't what they used to be, and probably never was.

—*Will Rogers*

Ever long for the good ol' days? 'Member the gang? Miss 'em? Boy, I do. You would too if you'da ever made out with Susie Jones in her living room with the music up loud and the lights down low while Dwight and Dixie and Jimmy and Ruth Ann all did likewise. Susie looked better with the lights down low. Dixie didn't need help. Poor Ruth Ann, she coulda used 'em a little lower.

'Member English Leather? Little square bottle of cologne with the fat top? Ever broke a jar of it all over you? Multiply that smell by three over-eager guys, and your nose is right in that living room with us. Poor girls were helpless, I'm tellin' ya. We're talkin' Smooch City. 'Sides, we had on our Levis and Madras plaid shirts, with fruit loops the girls would kill for.

Chuck? Oh, he was out with Sandra, or Carolyn, or Barbara. Not sure. Later that night though, at his house or mine, lying in bed, we'd swap stories 'til we fell asleep. "How'd you do? Did you kiss her? How's she kiss?"

We'd sleep in Saturday, eat breakfast, then be off to the football field or basketball court. Those days it was always something—girls, ball, guitars, late night, early AM talk sessions, hunting—something alla time. Chuck was one of my very best friends. We were so much alike.

I saw Chuck again, and his wife, one recent Friday night. He wasn't with Barbara, and I wasn't with Susie. Our wives hit it off better 'n Chuck and me. I felt that we were inspecting each other. I was him. He'd aged. Sure didn't look 17. Weighs 200 instead of 155. Thick mustache. Crown. Deep lines.

Philosophies? 23 years apart's a long time. He ordered a lite beer; I ordered root beer. He's a pilot; I'm a pastor. He doesn't go to church; I do. You can only talk about old times so long.

I'm sad. Will Rogers is right, I guess. "Things ain't what they used to be, and probably never was." On the other hand, maybe the writer of Ecclesiastes was right when he mused, "[God] has made everything beautiful in its time."

What do you think? Miss Chuck? Can you be thankful for the good ol' days without deifying those days? Chuck's great—my Chuck, your Chuck. Memory lane is hallowed ground. But why not look around you? Shouldn't joy be present tense? "The kingdom of God is at hand," Jesus said. Present. Like right now.

The next time I see Chuck, we'll probably relive the past, laugh, crack jokes. Then I think we'll celebrate and toast the truth from Ecclesiates: the good ol' days are now!

> *Do not say, "Why were the former days better than these?" For it is not from wisdom that you ask this. (Ecclesiastes 7:10)*

On Going Home Again

You can go home again. Things are just different when you do. That's all. Writing from my parent's home in McComb, Mississippi, seems normal enough. Dad rests in his easy chair. Mother cooks. I goof off. So what's different?

Much. Gone are the '57 Chevys, the ducktails, the bobby sox, the gang. Sue and Faye are grown and gone. No leather jackets, London Fogs, or Nehru coats. No cruising in my '64 Mustang. No madras plaid, or paisley, or "fruit loops," or bell bottoms.

Don and Chuck no longer live on Shelly Drive. Don's in San Antonio. Chuck's in Memphis. Lana's married and divorced. "Bonanza" is missing from TV. So is Ed Sullivan. Gone from radio are Elvis, Fabian, Fats Domino, the Everly Brothers, the Beatles, and the Supremes. So whatever happened to Motown, Herman's Hermits, and Louie Louie?

Gone is the draft, Vietnam, the Great Society, Kent State, and Bubba Walker. Nobody in McComb could shoot a basketball like Bubba Walker, or play drums like Jimmy Dale Hutto, or take National Merit tests like J. D. Fly, or look as good as Delilah Holmes.

Riding around McComb, I revisit the old hangouts, the "permanent" landmarks. The gym where I had my greatest year burned down. A vacant lot seems to taunt and say, "So?" Marking the spot where I was born stands a historic sign advertising parking for McDonald's.

Denman-Alford's, where I paid too much ($20) for Gant shirts in 1967, is closed. The East McComb Ice Cream Store, where my parents loved to treat my sisters and me, is boarded up. The water plant where my grandpa worked for years upon years has been torn down. My father's place of work for 40 years has been relocated, the old building I remember, deserted. Our old homeplace belongs to someone else. They bricked the house. So much for permanent landmarks. The old Greyhound bus station, once the site of civil rights violence and the refuge of COFO workers, is no more. In its place? The "Oasis." Sign says "Coldest Beer in Town."

First job I ever had was at Hollis' Drive-In as a skinny 13-year-old car hop. Mr. J. E. Thornhill always asked for two meat patties on his hamburger. Drove a yellow Cadillac. Hollis' is gone. Sign says "McComb Federal Credit Union."

I fell hopelessly in love with Haley Mills in *Pollyanna* at the Palace Theatre on Main Street. Main Street is still there; the Palace isn't. Neither is my old barbershop on Railroad Boulevard where I rode the horsey as a kid and got flattops as a teenager. My first date ever was to the State Theatre on State Street. It's closed. So is Pete Wade's Place, the honky-tonk my Dad once loved and I hated.

Remember the Blue & White Grill? I do. Dad and I would go there rather than to church on Sunday mornings. We'd drink cold chocolate milk and read the sports page. It's gone too. Gave way to the Bar-B-Que House. And the Oasis, where I played my first football card with Dad, is now a parking lot.

Just had to ride by Netterville Elementary School. There Miss Leblanc first taught me to love teachers and teaching. The school is closed, boarded up, windows out, paint peeling badly. Naturally, I suppose. Guess I should've expected it, too.

You can go home again. Things are just different. That's all. Oliver Emmerich, the brilliant and brave editor of our *Deep South* newspaper, has been deceased for years. And Dad's health is failing. Frankie Lynch, one of my favorite friends of childhood and adolescence, is dead. So is Prentiss Smith, a classmate I always liked. Went by their houses.

One last stop: my childhood church. How would it look? . . . The same. Unchanged. St. Andrew's United Methodist Church stands! Still doing those things that last. Still changing young lives with the Word of God. Thankfully, mine is one.

For B. P.

Thursday night, November 3, 1988, only seven seconds remain in their rival football game. Tishomingo High leads Faulkner 16–14. Due to tiebreaking rules, Tishomingo must win by 4 points or more to advance to the state playoffs.

Time for one last play. Tishomingo has the ball. A field goal will do it. But nobody in Tishomingo County, Mississippi, can kick a 52-yard field goal. "We weighed our chances and knew they weren't good," Coach Dave Herbert recalled. "We decided to go the other way."

Three cheers to Coach Herbert and his Tishomingo High School football team for taking a 65-yard safety! The self-inflicted safety tied the score 16–16 and sent the game into overtime. Tishomingo then scored and won 22–16 to advance to the state playoffs.

As one might imagine, the town of Tishomingo, population 500, all of whom at one time second-guessed their coach, is now pretty proud of him. But there is more to the story.

Coach Herbert called the play from a wheelchair on a flatbed truck parked along the sidelines. David Herbert, 46, has amyotrophic lateral sclerosis, better known as "Lou Gehrig's disease," a degenerative disease of the nerve cells that control muscular movement. The disease is deadly, and there is no known cure.

Two delay-of-game penalties were called against Tishomingo while the team murmured against and nearly mutinied over their coach's unusual call. "At first I thought it was crazy," quarterback Dave Herbert, the coach's son, recalled. "One guy even said Dad had lost his mind. But then I thought about it, and it made sense."

Hmmm . . . Wanna think about it awhile? Maybe life is kinda like a football game, and God is like Coach Herbert. Maybe sometimes it takes a safety to give us a chance at a touchdown. Who knows? Was not Christ's death on the cross, after all, a self-induced 65-yard safety? And what was the resurrection if not an overtime victory for the forces of good made possible by that safety?

Maybe God is up to something here. Seems we all fight the odds in life. We struggle, hanging in there bravely. Then something happens, something crazy, unexpected, an incredible setback. Bad call, God! Like the players at Tishomingo, we think the divine play-caller has lost His mind. Yet, our God has the final victory in view.

Along comes my friend, and God's child. And along comes retinitis pigmentosa, a degenerative disease of the retina marked by sclerosis and atrophy, cause unknown. Field of vision progressively decreases to blindness. A father, son, husband, doctor, Christian, friend, good man—why? Why should my friend go blind? The disciples questioned Jesus: "Rabbi, who sinned, this man or his parents?" Jesus answered: "Neither this man nor his parents sinned; he was born blind so that God's works might be revealed in him" (John 9:2-3).

There goes our coach again! I cannot say I understand God's every call; 65-yard safeties are hard to comprehend in any league. Even Coach Dave Herbert may testify that some setbacks in life are more easily understood than others. But apparently, our God calls the plays with a brilliant game plan in mind.

So, take heart teammates! Tishomingo, it appears, is only Indian for "Well, I'll be darned!" So the next time you're tempted to second-guess the guy with the sweatshirt and whistle in the sky, you might remember Tishomingo, Mississippi, where an inexplicable play glorified a local coach. Or you could just fall in behind B. P. as he glides by on his way to the real post-season play, as, once again, a coach is being glorified. . . . "Once I was blind, but now I see."

For we walk by faith, not by sight. (2 Corinthians 5:7)

Davy Crockett, Jim Bowie, and Barry Dale Dickerson

McComb had to be protected back in those days. Folks today, they forget what it was like back then. Not me. Times were tough in '55. Life, war. The women and children depended on us. Indians on the left. Indians on the right. Mexicans as thick as brick. Ammo running out. Blood oozing. No real place for the faint, the lame, the halt. Men only —real men, gallant men!

So we were only six years old! We were two cowboys that Injuns feared. Had no chance against—period, none. Battle after battle we claimed, heroically, for the forces of right in the face of overwhelming odds and at great personal peril. Hand-to-hand combat, exhaustion, loneliness commonplace.

Then it came. The moment we feared. The moment we were born for. Thousands upon thousands upon thousands they came: mean Mexican troops, as many as molecules. Led by the sinister Santa Anna they came. Just the two of us, Barry and me, against all odds. This was it, the Alamo. And we'd defend McComb to the last!

Barry had talked Aunt Billy Faye into buying him a coonskin cap. And he had it on. "I'm Crockett," he bragged. "You be Bowie." We looked at each other for what seemed like an eternity, then whispered, "Good luck."

1955. I do believe the greatest Injun fighter and Mexican fighter I ever saw, pound for pound, was cousin Barry Dale, "Davy Crockett," Dickerson. Yessir. Those were the days alright, days of war, of evil, of right, of sweat and courage; days of legend, days of lore.

Where have all the heroes gone? Cousin "Crockett" Dickerson is still battling evil forces as heroically as ever, championing the cause of Christ as pastor in the United Methodist Church in Mississippi. I'm proud to have fought beside that heroic six-year-old in the coonskin. I'm even prouder to fight beside him today against the spiritual hosts of Satan, not Santa Anna.

But alas, heroes age. Barry and I are not as young as we used to be. When a man's young and foolish, he thinks he can conquer the world, defend it, save it. A man turns seven, and he realizes he could use a little help in saving the world, after all.

For whatever it's worth, I got it on good authority that "Ol' Davy and Jim" are now accepting recruits for the cause, the cause of Christ, in the battle of our lives against spiritual forces named "legion." So how 'bout it? Any good men or women out there? Onward Christian soldiers! Sorry, you must be six or older to apply.

Endure hardship with us like a good soldier of Christ Jesus. (2 Timothy 2:3, NIV)

A Father-Daughter Story
Holding On, Letting Go
(A Journal Entry Written in Mexico)

Life is about letting go, rather than hanging on. Faith is, too. I know others argue that life is best lived with faith—and I agree—but that faith means "when you come to the end of your rope, you tie a knot and hang on."

I suppose that's one way of viewing faith and one way of approaching life. I would even admit that much of my own perspective has been similar. That is, in order to survive, I must be strong. What I do determines my well-being. Within me lies the stuff of triumph. By simply trying a little harder I can redirect my destiny. Ultimate power resides either in me or life's circumstances. Who/Which will prevail? How bad do you want it? Mind over matter. Competition. Control. Determination. Mountains move. Problems in the rear view. Victory parades you on its shoulders. Again, this "survival of the fittest" path is one I've trod, along with the rest of my species throughout time. How can one argue with Darwin, and what works? Perhaps one cannot.

But what if life in the spirit operates differently than life in the flesh? Was not Jesus saying that the kingdom of God and this world oppose each other in their principles of operation? That the way it is in one is not the way it is in the other?

So what does Jesus mean when he says, "Whoever loses his life for my sake will find it, and whoever keeps it will lose it"? What does he mean when he calls us "to deny ourselves, take up our cross, and follow him?" Isn't he inviting us to join him in traveling the road less taken? The path of self-denial rather than self-indulgence, to become givers not grabbers, to let go rather than hang on? Is this not the trail that leads to true life, true faith, and is, in fact, the only truth among the four-lane highways of lies and danger down which we speed with fuel and time running out? So I need to remember this, and not only to remember it but to live it.

When Alyson was two years-old and was diagnosed as having juvenile rheumatoid arthritis, I resisted, fought, hung on. But was that faith? And where was life? Only feelings of anguish, helplessness, pain, and pity—the stuff of hell—haunted my soul. Letting go, giving to God what was rightfully His—Alyson (and me)—changed the world. Night became day. Hell gave me up. Heaven came down. Grace and peace clothed me. Realizing that life wasn't "me versus the world," but that life is "God in the world" and "God with me and for me in His world," changed everything. I am not God. Alyson is not God. God is God. I am God's. Alyson is God's. Hanging on is idolatry. Letting go to God is letting God be God. I learn. But I forget.

So, now the mission trip we're on: 1995 rather that 1983. A 14-year-old daughter lives before my eyes; the two-year-old has grown up. The JRA gone. Time flies. Though I've gone on other mission trips for right reasons, and did this time, too, I hope, I confess that much of my excitement was at the prospect of spending quality time with Alyson. Things have been different than I expected, though very good nonetheless. Watching her interact with her peers has given me a window into her personality; watching her interact with the little Mexican children has given me a window into her character. Both are beautiful. I have enjoyed watching her immensely. I am exceedingly proud of her and absolutely in love with her. To think that God my Father feels the same about me touches me profoundly.

Ah, but her independence. She has hardly noticed that I'm here. On one hand I am overjoyed at her healthy adaptation to a family of significant others beyond our home. On the other hand, not feeling needed can be hard. It means I have to adjust. Alyson is growing up. I think I've grown back into holding on over the past twelve years. And it's hard. Always has been for me. Still is. But it's good, too. Life in the

Spirit is not one of control, but freedom. God's way is the only way, and I'm trying to say "Yes sir" again.

Yesterday, something beautiful happened. I will not soon forget it, if ever. Several of the youth decided to climb a mountain behind the village of O JO where we painted a church and took medical supplies. Alyson went, too.

The mountain was at places solely rock, but in other places sand had blown in deeply on top of the rock. Climbing was hard. Aly tired. Soon she was bringing up the rear. Others sped ahead. I told some back at the church as we watched from the distance that Alyson wouldn't make it—she would come back. She went a little further though, then again sat to rest. I still didn't think she would go on. Then one of the youth came back to aid Aly. Jeremy Lintz, who had been far ahead, came back to help Aly. He stayed with her, helping, encouraging, pulling, resting with her, as I watched from afar.

Immediately, I liked Jeremy. I would have liked him had the person he helped been another boy or someone else's daughter. What he did, who he is, is class. No, make that Christ. But it wasn't someone else he helped. He helped Alyson. I was proud. And thankful. Proud of Jeremy for helping. Proud of Alyson for going on. Thankful for Jeremy's heart. Thankful someone else would do what I would have done had I been there. Thankful God showed me that I can't always be there. And when I'm not, He is. This time, reflected in Jeremy. Next time somebody else. But always there. So I must let go. Let Alyson. Let Jeremy. Let God. Let go. I must let go. Life is about letting go. So is hope. So is faith. So is love.

Dear God, as you have let me go, may I let Alyson go. And may we both reward our Father's faith and love. Amen

The Hound of Heaven

Cletis Dover and his prized beagle, Judy, went hunting one Saturday morning hoping to bag a couple of rabbits. Instead, they treed two fugitives.

Dover, age 61 of Brinkley, Arkansas, was hunting in a wooded area outside of town when he came across the wanted men. "I just walked up on 'em. I recognized 'em from the television pictures," Dover related. "They had one of my dogs with 'em, patting her on the head." Authorities had been searching for the pair, wanted in Pennsylvania on kidnapping, rape, and murder charges.

Judy may not have caught a rabbit, but—Elvis' crooning to the contrary—she is a friend of mine. And though the fugitives, John Henretta and Michael Goodhart, may not exactly be found among Judy's litter of autograph hounds, who knows, perhaps they, too, may yet come to view her as used of God.

Francis Thompson, educated to be a physician, lived instead a destitute, drug-cursed vagabond's existence on the streets of London. Yet he penned "The Hound of Heaven," that famous poem of a sinner fleeing from the pursuing love of Christ. "I fled him, down the nights and down the days," Thompson wrote. "I hid from him, and under running laughter . . . From those strong feet that followed, followed after." Yet he heard Christ say, "All which I took from thee, I did but take, not for thy harms. But just that thou might'st seek it in my arms."

Judy found the fugitives. The fugitives found you can't hide from the long arm of the law. And Christ found Francis Thompson. So look out fugitives everywhere! I'm afraid the chase isn't over yet. Francis Thompson's "Hound of Heaven" is on your trail. And what about you? Are you running from God? You can run, but you can't hide.

The Son of Man came to seek out and to save the lost. (Luke 19:10)

To Your Health

No bacon, no jam, and no salt. Forget the eggs, sugar, chocolate, and caffeine. Cigs and alcohol? Taboo. Gone forever are T-bone steaks, liver, hamburgers, and decent milk. "Out" is my ol' favorite, the Snickers Bar. "In" is the rice cake.

The rule of thumb these days is "if it tastes like cardboard, eat it." Magic words? Fiber, roughage, grain. "If it tastes great, the grim reaper cooked it."

Books. *The 8-Week Cholesterol Cure.* Now there's a book with some delicious dishes. Yo Momma! Thin So Fast. Follow a few simple guidelines herein, and hear your friends, as you walk by, whispering in hushed tones: "Chemo," "How long?" "Anorexia," "AIDS," "Poor thing."

"Thin is in," they say. The C-word is cholesterol, found only in animal products. Translated forcefully: "Don't eat dead animals." "But I like dead animals—I mean red meat," you say. "Do and die," our experts reply.

Now they tell us there is good cholesterol and bad, HDL and LDL, high-density lipoproteins and low. And if I don't know the difference, my heart's gonna bust. Thanks.

What I really need, I'm told, is the Mediterranean diet: fish (broiled not fried), grains, veggies, and olive oil. Next comes a study that assures me three ounces of oat bran a day will lower my LDL's 23%. Mind if I ask you a personal question? How many ounces of oat bran can you eat without losing your lunch?

Not to worry, I'm told. "Mix it up. Eat all the broccoli, beans, fruit, grains, and hot cereals you want." But what if I've done that already," I wanna ask, "by the time I was four?"

Okay. So I confess. It's kinda hard changing lifetime eating patterns. Giving up my favorite foods. Adjusting to the diet decade. Seems most of us ol' boys prefer the monicker, "Tiger," over "Twiggy."

What about you? Where do you find yourself in all of this "health and fitness" business? Is your favorite Scripture, like mine, Leviticus 3:16, "All fat is the Lord's?" Any changes needed? If so, welcome to the club, Reverend Randall Love Handle, president. Better go for now. Supper's ready. The aroma of broccoli and oatmeal beckons.

But he that putteth his trust in the Lord will be made fat. (Prov 28:25, ERV)

The Secret of Life

The secret of man's being is not only to live but to have something to live for.

—*Dostoevsky*

In "The Myth of Sisyphus," the gods punish Sisyphus by making him roll a stone up a mountain. Just as he manages to reach the top, exhausted, the stone rolls back down the steep incline. This nightmare occurs again and again. Endless, futile, fruitless labor. Cruel labor imposed by the gods.

Camus argued that life is like that. He said that we are all Sisyphus. We eat, we work, we sleep. Or more precisely, we arise, eat, work several hours, eat, work some more, go home, eat, sleep, and start over again. Monday, Tuesday, Wednesday, Thursday, Friday (and sometimes Saturday and Sunday), we do this. We then have children, and they repeat the futile routine. Life has no meaning unless we make it have meaning, said Camus, or unless we at least find its meaning, a Christian might prefer to say.

Have you found ultimate meaning? For what or whom are you living? Why not try God? When Paul wrote, "Whatever gains I had, these I have come to regard as loss because of Christ" (Phil 3:7), he was saying, "I found it!" *Meaning, ultimate meaning!* Perhaps Paul could have said, "Once I was 'in Sisyphus,' but now, I am in Christ"—which translated means: "Let him who is without meaning roll the last stone."

Strive first for the kingdom of God and his righteousness, and all these things will be given you as well. (Matthew 6:33)

Goodness or Germs?

Picture this scenario: A friend whom you trust spreads harmful accusations about you. Rather than explode and respond with ill will, you pray for that person and speak lovingly of his or her good attributes. Then you are "rewarded" with increased protection from the next germ that comes your way.

Poppycock? Don't be so sure. Long ago, Jesus taught all who would listen the mysterious correlation between spiritual and physical wellness. "Hate or health . . . choose," he all but said. "Love and live," Jesus encouraged.

Now comes the result of recent scientific studies on the subject. Conclusion? The brain is more involved in physical health than ever before realized. And, a caring brain promotes good health!

In their book *The Healing Brain*, Drs. Robert Ornstein and David Sobel offer laboratory proof of the connection between goodness and wellness. For instance, David McClelland, Ph.D., Harvard, studied the effects that the good deeds of Mother Teresa had upon students who simply watched films of her in action with the poor. The results? Elevated levels of Immunoglobulin A (germ-fighting substance) in the students' saliva. On the other hand, studies revealed low levels of Immunoglobulin A in persons who need to dominate or control others.

Jesus said, "Love your enemies, do good to those who hate you. . . . Do to others as you would have them do to you. . . . For the measure you give will be the measure you get back" (Luke 6:27, 31, 38).

Certainly bad things happen to good people, as the book of Job and experience teach us. "Jesus or germs" may be carrying it too far. Nevertheless, it seems that both science and Scripture are trying to whisper to us humanoids a new old truth: something inherent in the human make-up needs to be good.

Seek good and not evil, that you may live. (Amos 5:14a)

Why Write a Book?

Write a book? Why would anyone want to write a book? Perhaps I should be as wise as Rabbi Menahem-Mendl of Kotzk.

"Do you know why I don't publish anything?" he asked a visitor. "I'll tell you why. Who would read me? Not the scientists, not the scholars; they know more than I do. To wish to read me, a man would have to feel that he knows less than I. Who might that be? A poor villager who works hard all week. When would he have time to open a book? On the Sabbath. When, at what time? Not at night; he would be too tired. Morning? Reserved for services. Following which, he comes home at midday, enjoys his meal, and rushes to lie down on his sofa, at peace with himself."

"Finally, he has a chance to glance at a book. He takes mine; he opens it. But he has eaten too much; he feels heavy. He gets drowsier by the minute; he falls asleep, and here is my volume falling from his hands. And is it for him—for that—that I should publish a book?"

Of making many books there is no end . . . (Ecclesiastes 12:12b)

Antiques *and* Tattoos?

It's there. I kid you not. Travel north on I-55 from New Orleans to Ponchatoula, and you'll see it. Just before you reach Ponchatoula. Right side of the road. White square sign. Bold black letters. "ANTIQUES and TATTOOS." Oooh . . . Tough choice. "Which do I want today? An oak hall tree or a naked lady on my bicep?"

"'Cuse me ma'm. How much is your roll-top desk? $1,895.00? Thank you. And how much are the lovely tattoos did you say? $22.50? I see. Bargain. Thank you. Ma'm, oh ma'm, just one more question if I could. I hate to ask this, but do you think y'all could tattoo a roll-top desk on my belly so when I suck it in like this, the top closes; but when I poke out my stomach like this, the top rolls back? Ma'm? Oh yes ma'm, I'd love to have the roll-top, sure would. It's just that I'm afraid the lovely tattoo is more in my price range today. Thank you ma'm, I like your store."

Can you believe it? What am I missing here? Antiques and Tattoos? Same store? I give up. You take a turn. I'll say a word. You say the first thing that comes to mind. Antiques: "grandparents." Okay. Good. Tattoos: "gypsies." Good. Antiques: "connection to the past." Tattoo: "free, baby, free." Antiques and Tattoos: "Ma and Pa versus Motorcycle Momma and Cool Daddy." Very good. You're catching on. See what I mean?

What's wrong with this picture? On one hand: nostalgia, sentiment, cherished memories, white picket fences, farmhouses, cast-iron beds, old photo albums, and oval picture frames. On the other hand: rebellion, rootlessness, booze, drugs, motorcycles, and fights. How could one place of business possibly cater to such divergent clientele? Aunt Bea shops for antiques while Hell's Angels get tattoos. See what I mean? It won't work. It couldn't! . . . Could it?

Just thinking, but could the church stand to be a little more "open for business" to all comers, including the tattoo crowd? Do we not show strong partiality to the good citizens of the antiques circle? "But if you show partiality, you commit sin" (Jas 2:9). Could we better peddle the gospel to all potential customers—rich and poor, clean and unclean?

If you think about it, church really is a place where one can get both his "antiques" and "tattoos" needs met. What is the cross if not mother's and daddy's and grandma's and grandpa's and great-grandma's heirloom of salvation to which we are all heir? So you like antiques? How 'bout that 1779 hymn, "Amazing Grace"? "Just Gimme That Ol' Time Religion."

Tattoo crowd happy at church? And why not? "Born to be free," are you? Meet Jesus Christ. "You will know the truth, and the truth will make you free" (John 8:32).

Tattoos? "I will write [my law] on their hearts" (Jer 31:33). "Bind them [God's words] as a sign on your hand, fix them as an emblem on your forehead" (Deut 6:8) "You are a letter of Christ . . . written not with ink but with the Spirit of the living God . . . on . . . human hearts" (2 Cor 3:3).

So how 'bout it? Whoever you are, wherever you are, whatever your need, you really don't have to drive to Ponchatoula, Louisiana, to have your needs met this weekend. You could try church. Never know. God just might have what you're looking for. At the Gospel Store "antiques and tattoos" are free. A relative of yours paid in full and left them for you in his name.

God's Tummy

One Monday night in March 1987, we were having family devotional time following supper. We read about creation, Adam and Eve, the Garden. Alyson, age six, asked, "How could God make us? Our eyes, our noses, our faces? Not just now but then, at first! How did God make Adam and Eve?

There were no mommies for babies to come from." Shannon, not yet four, replied, "Adam and Eve came from God's tummy, Alyson." "But God is a man," Alyson responded. "So how could they, Shannon?"

Kay and I asked Alyson if she were sure that God is a man. She answered, "Yes, I think so. Besides, Jesus was a man, and he was God." We tried to explain that God was Spirit. Shannon was having no part of it. She insisted that God was a man. "Oh? And why do you say so?" we asked. "Cause of His name," she reasoned. "Did you ever hear of a girl named God?"

. . . The Almighty will bless you with blessings of heaven above, . . . blessings of the breasts and of the womb. (Genesis 49:25)

An Irish Prayer

May those who love us love us,
and for those who do not love us,
May God change their hearts,
If not, may He turn their ankles,
So that we may know them by their limping.

. . . Lord, teach us to pray . . . (Luke 11:1)

ENCOURAGEMENT

Coach Scores Big

Have you ever failed miserably when everyone was counting on you? Have you ever wanted to succeed so badly that defeat totally devastated you? Have you ever felt so humiliated that you were left without a sense of worth?

I have. Maybe we all have. Perhaps we've all been Charlie Brown. Have you ever struck out in baseball in the last inning, runners on base, trailing by one run, everyone cheering loud encouragement, breathing quiet prayers? I have. Have you ever missed the game-winning shot in basketball, the hail-Mary pass in football, or even missed making the team? Me, too. I have also known academic failure, moral failure, and interpersonal failure. But the worse pain from failure I have ever felt I suffered vicariously. There is no pain like the agony we feel when our children hurt.

Christopher, our seven-year-old son, loves sports. Unfortunately, he did not win the genetic lottery. You know the saying, "If you want to be a great athlete, choose your parents carefully." Poor Chris.

In a T-ball game, before God and everybody, Christopher struck out. That's hard to do since the ball sits stationary on a stand. To make matters worse, Chris is one of the oldest players on his team, having played last year. He had always feared striking out, said he never would, and, in fact, never had, until yesterday.

Swing and a miss. "Strike one!" Swings again. Hits the stand, not the ball. "Strike two!" Tries harder. Nothing but air. "Strike three, you're out!" Crying in shame, Chris runs to his mother and tries to disappear from the planet. I'm coaching first base, suffering with him helplessly from a distance. Somehow his mother coaxes him back onto the field where he plays his heart out defensively, chasing the ball in the outfield, making determined throws back in.

Next time up to bat? "Strike one! Strike two! Strike three, you're out!" Can one try too hard? Third time up? Horrors!

Instant replay. Concentration, determination, prayer aside, "Strike three, you're out!" Oh, the humiliation.

I can't describe Christopher's pain, nor mine for him. Words fail. As Chris buried his head in his mother's embrace, crying in shame again, we all hurt—the whole crowd. "I'll never, ever come back again," he wept. Who could blame him?

As the team gathered around their coach for the customary post-game words, Coach Paul Anderson congratulated the team for a great effort. "As you know, we always award a game ball to our most valuable player each game. Today, I'm awarding two game balls. The first one goes to Thomas Long for his hitting. The second game ball goes to a player who starred on defense, was all over the ball, and played his hardest: Christopher O'Brien!"

I lost it. 'Fact, I'm still choked up. You should've seen my little guy's spirit soar. New life erupted. The sun danced. The trees sang. Resurrection.

As Christopher ran off with his teammates to the concession stand, clutching his game ball, I intercepted his coach. "You are one class act, my friend. Thank you for what you did," I exclaimed. Looking him straight in the eye, speaking slowly, I vowed, "I will never forget this as long as I live. How can we ever thank you?"

"Don't mention it," he said. But I am. I also want to mention one other thing. Yesterday I found two new heroes: my son and my son's coach.

(P.S. Two games later, guess who had three hits, including *a home run*? Way to go Chris! And Coach, again, *thanks!*)

Do not withhold good . . . when it is in your power to do it. (Proverbs 3:27)

Angel Unaware?

Pastoring a church is difficult. Most jobs are. Church work is no exception. In fact, the pastorate contains five full-time jobs rolled into one: administration, outreach and evangelism, counseling, pastoral care, and study and preaching.

No one has more than 100% of his time: $100 \div 5 = 20$. Pastors can only give 20% or less of their time to each of their five jobs. Left unmentioned is time for God, spouse, children, or self. There are just so many hours in the day.

Perfectionists struggle in the ministry. One has no choice but to learn to live with the incomplete. The work is never done, nor done well enough to suit everyone. Some want the pastor to be a better administrator. Some insist that the pastor spend more time in pastoral care. Others note that the church isn't growing as fast as Donald Trump's empire. Still others complain about pulpit performance, substance or style, or both.

Ministers may give all of their time (the 20% allotment) to each aspect of the job only to realize that the other 80% of the job went undone that day, that week. The other four jobs prevent their doing more. They can agree with their critics, yet find course correction difficult, if not impossible. With this introduction comes the following story.

The fall of 1989 saw my spirits drop, like the leaves that fell from the colorful Little Rock trees undressing for the deathly look of winter. Winter was blowing into my soul. Despair chilled my heart. It seemed impossible to pastor my church as need demanded, or at least it seemed impossible for me to do so anyway. I began to question my call from God. No pastor serves without critics. I had mine. Perhaps they were right. Maybe I should move on, try something else or try it somewhere else. My harshest critic? Me! I had never given myself permission to fail. A perfectionist, I now saw, painfully, my imperfections. I felt that I was failing. I was considering quitting preaching that fall. "Maybe I'm in the wrong business," I lamented. I began thinking about possibly doing other things, maybe buying a small town newspaper, trying to serve my fellow man that way. Life hurt. Questions loomed.

Some good friends gave Kay and me two tickets to a big college football game. I couldn't wait! Just to get away with Kay for a weekend would be healing. Then the phone rang. Long distance. "He passed away this morning. Could you preach the funeral Saturday?" I didn't even know him. Met him once. The game? What about the game? I'd miss the big game.

Driving the several hours to the funeral site afforded me the dark occasion to throw a pity party—big time, guest list of two: misery and me. Of course, once there, I ministered to the family, then did my best at the funeral service. At last we all got into our cars and rode forever through the countryside, miles upon miles, until we turned onto a narrow gravel road that snaked its way to a lovely cemetery on top of a hill in the middle of nowhere Arkansas.

I uttered my piece, committed the deceased to his resting place, paid my final respects to the family, then turned to walk toward my car. The walk was a long one, over the hill, down the winding road. I was almost at my car when a voice called.

"Preacher, oh Preacher!"

Stopping and turning, I saw a figure approaching in the distance.

"Preacher, got just a minute?"

I waited.

"Preacher, that was a mighty fine funeral sermon you gave."

"Thank you very much," I replied, "you're very kind."

"Look, Preacher, there's something that I have to say to you."

"Sure, go ahead," I ventured.

"I didn't know the deceased," he whispered.

"Neither did I," I whispered back.

"I just felt like I had to come here today," he continued.

"So did I," I confessed.

"I'm not from around here," the mysterious figure shared.

"Neither am I," I countered.

"Look, there's something I've just got to say to you" he stated strongly while looking me straight in the eye. "I've got to tell you this."

Silence.

"*Whatever* you do," he paused, "Whatever you do . . . Whatever you do, don't you ever, ever, . . . *ever* stop preaching."

Speechless I stood, silently I watched, as my mysterious visitor from who-knows-where turned and disappeared over the hill.

. . . Some have entertained angels without knowing it. (Hebrews 13:2)

🐝 🐝 🐝

My Most Memorable Deacon

Vietnam lay behind me, as Egypt lay behind the Hebrews. The shadows of death had disappeared before the dazzling light of freedom. God had delivered me. What the Bastille had meant to the French, the Bolshevik Revolution was to the Russians, and the Exodus had been to the Israelites, so Vietnam was to me. Freedom. Peace. New life. Literally, but more importantly, spiritually.

Although I had been a Christian since childhood, like many others, I had wandered aimlessly away as a teenager. The rebellious teen years were, for me, not totally unlike "being in Egypt." The oppression of guilt and the bondage to sin left me, though a child of God, enslaved in a "far country." Then, running from God, I had volunteered to fight in Vietnam.

God found me! As God found the Israelite children in Egypt and also the prodigal son, God found me. In the land of Vietnam, during the height of war, I gave my life totally to

God through Jesus Christ. Thus from the land of Vietnam and the state of sin, God delivered me. I came home.

Upon my return to South Mississippi in 1971, I was "on fire for Christ." Wherever and whenever opportunities arose for me to share my personal testimony for Jesus Christ, I did so enthusiastically. Speaking to youth groups, college groups, and in churches of any denomination, I shared the good news of Christ's life-changing love and grace. My small church soon asked me to serve as volunteer youth minister. I eagerly accepted.

Then the crisis hit. An evangelist came to town preaching that if someone did not know when they were saved, they very well may be lost. As we sang, he would shout, "Stand if you were saved on a Monday." Then he would go on to Tuesday and Wednesday, etc. He warned, "If you don't know when you were saved, maybe you weren't." Then he added for evidence, "I remember the date, the day, and the time I was saved as plainly as though it were yesterday."

I began to doubt my salvation. Maybe I had never been born again. I could remember my baptism as a child, but not my day of salvation. After the evangelist left our town, my troubles only persisted. The doubting and confusion were painful. How could I serve God in this condition?

Meet Louie Smith. Were you to see him, you might not be overly impressed. "Uncle Louie," as we all called him, must have been in his 70s. He was bald, slow moving, average height, and always modestly attired. As far as I knew, he had always been a farmer.

Uncle Louie was a deacon in our church and our volunteer songleader in worship services. His pride and joy, the absolute love of Uncle Louie's life, was "Miss Myrtis," his "bride," as he called her, of some 50 years. I loved them dearly.

Uncle Louie had a quiet peace about him that made me feel at ease. As my anguish reached its peak, I decided to drive to Uncle Louie's and pour out my heart to him. There, in the cozy warmth of their small living room, with "Miss

Myrtis" rocking and knitting and Uncle Louie and I seated by the fire in chairs, I let it all out.

Uncle Louie just listened. When at last I finished my story, he looked at me, eyes twinkling, and asked, "Do you believe I love Miss Myrtis, Son?"

Of course I believed Uncle Louie loved Miss Myrtis. Everybody knew that. Why else would he still be opening car doors for her after 50 years of marriage? Why else did he still refer to her as his "bride?" "Yes sir," I replied, "I know you love Miss Myrtis."

"How do you know that?" he asked. I told him. He chuckled. Then he and Miss Myrtis laughed lovingly, almost sheepishly, as though I had caught them in an inside joke. Then he told me their mutually embarrassing confession. "The other day Miss Myrtis and I were sitting right here trying to remember when it was that we met. Do you know when that was?"

"No, sir, I don't," I answered.

"Neither do we," he laughed.

We all laughed. "For the life of me," he shook his head and confessed, "I can't remember when I first met Miss Myrtis or when it was that we first fell in love. But let me ask you something, Son. Do you believe I love Miss Myrtis?"

I was beginning to catch on when he became as serious as I ever saw Uncle Louie. He leaned forward in his chair, looked me straight in the eye, and said, "Son, listen to me. I know you love Jesus. I know you love Jesus the same way you know I love Miss Myrtis. A lot of us can't remember the exact day of things, but the Good Book says you will know a tree by the fruit it bears even if you don't remember when it was you planted it."

I left Uncle Louie's that day a new person; 25 years of ministry later, I have never again doubted my salvation. Recently, however, a preacher-friend of mine was struggling in a midlife crisis, aggravated by the excruciating anguish of doubting his salvation. A well-intentioned revival preacher had caused him and several others in the church such spiritual uncertainty that counseling was required for my friend.

One day my friend traveled to see me, to visit, and to pour out his heart. I listened reverently. When he had finished his story, I smiled and asked, "Do you believe I love Kay?" And so our conversation unfolded as I prayerfully "played Uncle Louie."

Today my friend is still preaching and doing well. Uncle Louie? He went home to be with his Lord and his "bride" a few years ago. However, I do believe it is safe to say, as long as I live, Uncle Louie will go on "deaconing" to God's children.

> *For those who serve well as deacons gain a good standing for themselves and great boldness in the faith that is in Christ Jesus. (1 Timothy 3:13)*

Billy Bloomfield's Wet Britches

You laugh, but you never saw Bubba Walker. And even if you did, you never saw him throw a baseball. We did—plenty of times. Billy Bloomfield sure did.

Bubba was a large human—Goliath's big brother. Even when he was little, he was big. He would go on to star in two sports as a 6'4" dominant athlete at McComb High. Then off to State on full scholarship.

Bubba reached manhood somewhere around 12, just prior to his last year of Little League baseball, as I recall in a cold sweat. Dragon size, maybe bigger—age 12.

Which brings me back to Billy Bloomfield. We all dreaded batting against Bubba Walker. No exceptions. 'Course we all tried to hide it. I hate to say we were scared to death of Bubba, but we were scared to death of Bubba. The man threw so hard that the catcher wore a sponge in his mit!

Usually, when we had to bat against Bubba, we'd do five things: (1) cry; (2) pray; (3) swing at the first three pitches; (4) go back to the dugout and pray, beg, "Please Lord, let Coach put someone in my place. I'll be a preacher—anything"; and (5) think of ways to gracefully quit the game forever.

Poor Billy. Had his new white uniform on and everything, that hot summer day in '58. Praying in the batter's box helps. Billy was praying. Bubba went into his windup. And Billy went in his pants.

Poor Billy Bloomfield. We all saw it—the girls, guys, parents, ump, Bubba—everybody. We all saw it. The dark, large, wet, expanding circle against the otherwise bright white dry pants. Poor Billy Bloomfield. What can you say in times like that? "Excuse me"?

Woe is me. Life is like that. Billy could be any of us. Secretly, are we not all scared to death of facing Bubba? . . . The next grade in school, leaving home, getting married, responsibility for providing adequately for others, new job, social interaction, finding the meaning of life, aging, death and dying . . . Bubba throws hard.

And we try to hide our secret fears, don't we? Well, Billy couldn't. But Billy is my hero. Why? 'Cause everybody in McComb knew Billy Bloomfield wet his britches. Yet Billy hung in there. Never quit. Faced the fiddler. Everyday. Going through life's beltline.

Courage. That's what I call it. That's what life takes. And character. Heroes. That's who you are. All you folks out there standing in the batter's box everyday against Bubba. With courage and character you stand in there. When life scares you to death, humiliates you, laughs at you publicly, still you stand. "For God did not give us a spirit of cowardice, but rather a spirit of power and of love and of self-discipline" (2 Tim 1:7).

No, Billy Bloomfield never made it to the Major Leagues. You might not either. But if ever they name an All-McComb, All-Time baseball team based on courage and character, I think I've got a nominee. Eight batters after he soiled his suit in front of God and everybody, guess who stepped back into the batter's box?

So what about you? Life treating you roughly? Scared? Tired? Ever feel like quitting? Who knows? One day someone, somewhere just might name an all-world, all-time team of unsung heroes. So, hey, hey, what d'ya say? Batter up?

Bulldogs or Dalmatians?

A once-in-the-history-of-the-game phenomenon occurred in baseball at the close of the 1988 season. A professional pitcher hurled an unprecedented 59 consecutive scoreless innings, for 7 incredible shutout victories, in only 46 days!

Then, after pitching, and winning, half of his team's games in the World Series, he coolly claimed coveted MVP honors. Add to these accomplishments his World Series record (tied) 1,000 batting average, and you see why the other teams spent the off-season looking for kryptonite.

Meet Orel Hershiser, a.k.a. (also known as) "Bulldog." Now get this. Just what do you think "Bulldog" does to handle his world record stress, as he faces and mows down endless enemy batters who challenge him? He sings hymns. Can you believe it? Bulldog sings hymns such as "Praise God from Whom All Blessings Flow" while he's actually pitching!!

Don't you just love it? I can't help but wonder if my own record of facing and mowing down challenges might not sparkle more brightly, were I, too, to sing God's praises, even in the tough times. But not just in the tough times, mind you. Too many of us do that already. "Dalmatian" Christians we might call ourselves—religious in spots. Nor should we praise God only in the good times. Right, dalmatians again.

The early Christians, were, of course, the original bulldogs—year-round tough! They sang hymns and praised God in all times, good or bad. Even in prison, "Paul and Silas were praying and singing hymns to God" (Acts 16:25). The apostle Paul, himself quite a feisty breed and major league pitcher of the gospel nonpareil, advised: "Rejoice always, pray without ceasing, give thanks in all circumstances; for this is the will of God in Christ Jesus for you" (1 Thess 5:16-18).

Just thinking . . . but if Orel Hershiser can pitch seven shutouts against forces seeking to defeat him, and if he literally draws strength from hymns of praise, and if Paul and Silas could pray and sing hymns and turn a prison into a revival, then what are we waiting for?

Guess only one question remains: Will we be Dalmatians or Bulldogs? Amazing g-r-r-owl—I mean, grace.

Give thanks in all circumstances. (1 Thessalonians 5:18a)

Toward a Theology of Testimony

Johann Sebastian Bach was described by no less an authority than Beethoven as "an ocean of creativity compared to whom all other composers were mere brooks." Brahms would miss meals in order to study Bach's latest musical compositions. With so lofty a testimony to Bach's greatness as these words and ways from the great composers Beethoven and Brahms, what more could possibly be said about this master musician? (Clue: try the musician's Master).

Did you know that Bach initialed his completed compositions, "S. D. G." (*Soli Deo Gloria*—"To God alone be the glory")? And on occasion he would begin by writing, "J. J." (*Jesu juva*—"Jesus, help me").

All who knew Johann Sabastian Bach knew of his love for his Lord Jesus. Can the same be said of us? In particular, I must wonder what kind of witness we have where our influence is greatest: in our home and with our friends.

A recent poll indicates that as many as 90% of the people in church are active because of the testimony and influence of family members or friends. Only 1 out of 8,000 was converted through an evangelistic crusade, and only 2 out of 100 through visitation programs. Crusades and door-to-door evangelism are not to be abandoned. But studies show that "friendship evangelism," where persons are important and relationships are treasured, serve God best.

You and I are rather unlikely to have Bach's international forum to testify for Christ. At one point, however, the apostle Paul boasted that some believers were his letter, his composition, "written on our hearts . . . and you show that you are a letter of Christ . . . written not with ink but with the Spirit of the living God" (2 Cor 3:2-3).

Think about it. Is God saying that you and I could become composers, literary not musical, spiritual not literal? Might there be a special someone who could become your letter for Christ, . . . upon whose soul you could initial "S. D. G.?" *Jesu juva*!

Holy Water

Serving as pastor of Calvary Church in Little Rock, Arkansas, was the busiest time of my life. Some say, "Busy is the profanity of the church today." We're all too busy, aren't we?

Work weeks of 70 to 90 hours were not uncommon for me; family time was. The dog growled at me when I came home. The children had to be introduced to me. And Kay and I were ships passing in the night.

We agreed that something had to be done. We bought a boat, a pontoon boat. Party barge. Perfect for family fun. Picnics on the water. Swimming. Laughing. Playing. Cooking. Pulling kids on inner tubes. Relaxing in the sun.

Tom and Betty Miller had a cabin on Lake Hamilton 30 miles away in Hot Springs. They were angels sent to our family. "Why don't you leave your boat at our cabin on the lake? We'll give you a key. Just go over anytime you want."

The kids were excited. Kay was excited. I was excited. Problem was, I couldn't get away. The picture looked bleak. I mean, what do you tell the needy when they call? The lame, the blind, the halt? Inquiring church members and probing deacons? "Sorry, the pastor is chilling out behind his Ray Bans working on his tan."

One of the children had a brainstorm. "We need to name the boat, Daddy." "Name the boat?" I asked. "Why?" They giggled and whispered in my ear. Soon we were all laughing. Ever hear of a boat named *Visitation*?

The next gorgeous sun-splashed day, as the calls poured in like clockwork, the church secretary explained, "I'm sorry, our pastor is out on visitation."

And after he had dismissed the crowds, he went up to the mountain by himself . . . (Matthew 14:23)

Aesop Meets Cyclops

An Old Crab said to her son, "Why do you walk sideways like that, my son? You ought to walk straight." The Young Crab replied, "Show me how, dear Mother, and I'll follow your example." The Old Crab tried, but in vain, and then saw how foolish she had been to find fault with her child.

As you know, Aesop's fables are a collection of legendary tales about animals and birds that cleverly expose our universal human weaknesses. And, as you might recall, in Greek mythology a Cyclops was any of a race of giants having only one eye in the middle of the forehead.

Well, recently I have been rather overbearing with our children. Just this week, in fact, I was ranting and raving. "These rooms are a mess! Why can't you girls keep your rooms clean? This looks terrible!" "But Daddy," Alyson responded, "remember the crab story?" "Yeah, Daddy," Shannon chimed in, "how can we walk straight if you don't show us?" "Daddy, your room is messy too," they observed in unison. (In the lingo of their daddy's trade, this move is called "applying the text.")

Okay. Ouch. No, the truth didn't hit me between the eyes; I've only got one. Sometimes I wonder if we adults aren't like Cyclops to our children: giants with only one eye, seeing all their shortcomings but minus the other eye to see our own.

Thanks to two wonderful little girls who love both Aesop and Cyclops, something good happened this week at 94 El Dorado. Aesop met Cyclops. And we all won. Blessings on your home!

Why do you see the speck in your neighbor's eye, but do not notice the log in your own eye? (Matthew 7:3)

"Get Me to the Church on Time" Takes on New Meaning

(reprinted from the *Arkansas Gazette*, April 1988)

Kay and Randall O'Brien could not remember a more pleasant or leisurely Easter Sunday morning. Randall O'Brien is pastor at Calvary Baptist Church. Their daughters, Alyson, seven, and Shannon, four, found their beautiful Easter baskets. They enjoyed a wonderful egg hunt. Then the family breakfast. Perfect.

The girls got dressed, picture pretty, and posed for snapshots. Randall O'Brien retired to the shower to get ready for the biggest service in his 10 months at Calvary Church.

It was 7:23, almost an hour before the early worship service. That was when the blood-curdling scream tore through the shower door. What Mr. O'Brien had not heard was the ringing of the telephone. On the line was Milt Loftis, a Calvary deacon and choir member.

Deacon Loftis said good morning to Kay O'Brien and asked about the minister. "Has he left the house yet?" Kay said no, as a matter of fact, her husband was enjoying a shower. Deacon Loftis said it in measured tones: "Kay, did you all forget to set your clocks forward?"

That's when Mrs. O'Brien screamed. There's no point in spelling out the frantic details. The best Randall O'Brien remembers, Kay stuffed his suit through the door while somebody started drying his hair and somebody else, maybe the preacher himself, started slipping shoes on his feet.

When he finally got to the year's biggest service, the choir had been singing one more verse for 45 minutes. The minister's parting words to his wife were in the form of a question: "Where would you like to spend next Easter?"

For everything there is a season, . . . a time to weep, and a time to laugh. (Ecclesiastes 3:1, 4a)

The Thinker

Our daughter Shannon is a bright kid. I like to say, "She has her daddy's mind." Her mother likes to be a wiseguy and crack, "She must. Her mother still has hers." Don't laugh. It's not funny. Besides, can I help it if my gene pool doesn't have a deep end?

Anyway, back to Shannon. Her name means "little wise one." Funny how names can be prophecies, isn't it? The first time we read *Cinderella* to Shannon, she had a problem with the story. Barely six years old, and she had major problems with Cinderella. "Why Daddy," she asked, "does everything in the story turn back to what it was at midnight, except the glass slipper?" Just like that she nuked Cinderella. No glass slipper, no storyline. . . . The story is dead, I'm saying—deceased.

She was only seven when we were having a family devotional one evening before bedtime. As the family listened to the story of Noah and the ark, Shannon interrupted: "Daddy, I've got a question." "Yes, Honey, what is it?" "Daddy, why didn't the dove come back?" "Good question, Sugar. That's a real good question. Let Daddy try to answer that for you. You see, the dove found land, the top of the mountain, so Noah knew the flood was over when the dove didn't return to the ark," I explained. "No Daddy, I understand that," she said. "Why didn't the dove come back for its mate? How do we have doves today, Daddy?" "Uh, time for you kids to get in bed! Hun, you wanna tuck 'em in tonight? Run along now," I insisted. "Get moving. Remember to say your prayers."

When I was a boy, my dad would sometimes stump me with brainteasers. Once as Shannon and I were riding in the family car, one came to mind. I decided to have some fun. "Are you ready for a riddle?" I challenged. "Sure," she responded unsuspectingly. "Okay," I teased, knowing I had her. "What happens when a force that cannot be stopped meets an object that cannot be moved?" I had her, and I knew it. It's an impossible equation. Nobody can answer it.

Immediately she responded, "How high is the object, like if it's a wall? And how long?" Checkmate. The child answered an unanswerable question. What a marvelous little mind! The Gospel according to Shannon reminds me that Christ came to take away our sins, not our minds.

In my study sits "The Thinker." You've seen the unclothed sculpture: chin in right hand, right elbow resting on left knee, contemplative pose struck. Shannon, age six, walked into my study where she found me reading at my desk. Studying the thinker for a moment, she asked, "Daddy, what's he thinking?" Well, now after awhile you learn. So I turned the tables. "That's a good question, Honey. I don't know. What do you think he's thinking?" A short pause then this: "I think he's thinking, 'Now where did I leave my clothes?'"

You shall love the Lord your God with all your heart, and with all your soul, and with all your mind. (Matthew 22:37)

Flowers or Fairness?

Three thousand years ago our mothers, daughters, and sisters possessed few rights. Society? Male-dominant. In the time of Moses, for instance, only men could inherit.

According to Numbers 27, Zelophehad died, leaving behind no sons. His five daughters approached Moses asking, "Why should the name of our father be taken away from his clan because he had no son? Give to us a possession among our father's brothers."

Now no one had ever thought of that before. Moses, it seems, was in over his head on this one. So he said to the girls, "Say what, sisters? Lemme check this out with God and get back with you first thing in the morning."

Some said it thundered. God spoke to Moses saying, "The daughters of Zelophehad are right . . . let them possess an inheritance."

*****

In May 1984, it seems a 10-year-old girl from Iowa City graciously turned down a scholastic award from the local Optimist Club because the group didn't allow women as members.

Charity Grant, a fourth-grader at Longfellow Elementary School, declined the "reading award." "It's like a bunch of silly little boys playing a game and not letting us girls play, too," she said in an interview.

School authorities were upset with Charity's action, defending the organization for "doing good." "I wanted the prize badly," Charity said, "but I thought it over and decided it would be a bigger prize to help stop discrimination against women."

Executive secretary, Hugh Cranford, of Optimist International in St. Louis, Missouri, replied that women were not permitted to join the club because "our constitution prohibits it."

"I remember sitting up in my bedroom and thinking, 'Who cares? Why shouldn't I take the prize?' " Charity related. "But I thought some more and decided I shouldn't take this award if they're discriminating against women."

*****

Ah, Mother's Day. So what of it? Well guys how 'bout it? What will it be this time? Flowers for a day or fairness to stay? . . . And some said it thundered.

... There is no longer male and female; for all of you are one in Christ Jesus. (Galatians 3:28)

🐝 🐝 🐝

The Super Bowl Shout

He was tuned in to every word. 'Twas January 22, 1989, and I was preaching hard that Sunday night. Super Bowl Sunday.

Since he was 85 years old, he would customarily sit on the church pew electronically equipped with earphones for the hard-of-hearing. So there he was, faithfully in his place, headset on, following me, eyeball to eyeball, listening to every word that night.

"Oh yeah!" he shouted, catching me and the congregation off guard just as I made a point in my sermon. His exuberance may have surprised even him a little. I couldn't tell. But the support surely fired me up!

After the service, as I was feeling pretty good about my sermon, my elder friend came to me and apologized, "Preacher, I'm sorry for hollering out like that." Before I could, on the contrary, express my gratitude, he continued. "It's just that ol' Joe Montana threw that ball to that Rice fellow. And, can you believe it, he took them 49ers all the way down that field? And did you know, those boys came from behind to beat that other bunch 20–16?"

Care to guess the headset of choice for our super friend? Those were *not* our earphones for the hearing impaired after all, but his own transistor radio headset! So much for "amens" during my sermons.

Wonder why? The earliest fans were in Jerusalem, not San Francisco or Dallas. The saints, not the 49ers or Cowboys, were the real fanatics. They played against lions in Rome, in the first Super Bowl ever.

I know fans today are devoted, but taking off shirts and painting bodies hardly compare to taking off heads and tearing bodies. What happened? Personally, I too received a thrill watching Joe "Big Sky" Montana, but I'm in total awe of the One who made the sky over Montana.

Why then the roar of the stadium versus the silence of the church? Who knows? But even my Super Bowl friend didn't shout until his team was on the move, which translated means: We fans may want to arrive early this Sunday at church. God's people are on the move.

You never know. This just might be the day when the saints go marching in, and marching out, praising God and doing the Super Bowl shout. Go saints!

Make a joyful noise to God . . . (Psalm 66:1)

A Story for the Children

Once upon a time there lived a gorgeous, multicolored, breathtaking unicorn. Everyone said, "How beautiful is the rainbow unicorn!" But, alas, she acted ugly, mean, and would never play with the children. Neither would she give them rides through the air, though the girls and boys pleaded, "Please, rainbow unicorn. Please take us for a ride through the air." Instead, the moody unicorn would sometimes snort and stomp and even splash mud on the children's clean clothes. And some of the kids would cry.

There lived nearby another unicorn, not very pretty, scarred and green, kind of ugly really, but very kind and sweet to the girls and boys. The ugly unicorn would give rides to the boys and girls. He would even rub against them and lick their hands. But some of the people made fun of the little unicorn, laughing, "Look how ugly the dumb animal is! Ha, ha, ha! How ugly!"

Then one day something strange happened, something unexpected, something wonderful! Some people say this happens only once every thousand years; some say it never ever really happens, that it's just make-believe; while others believe it could happen again today.

On this magical day they went to the stream to drink, the rainbow unicorn and the little ugly unicorn. And then it happened. While drinking and viewing their reflection in the water, a miracle occurred. The rainbow unicorn turned green, unshapely, ugly. The green, ugly unicorn became brightly colored, rainbow-like. Each turned on the outside what they were on the inside. And the whole wide world began to see them the way they acted: beautiful and ugly.

The happy little unicorn was so elated! Excitedly she found her little friends, all the girls and boys who had ever felt ugly or fat or skinny or left out or made fun of. And she taught them to sing:

> *Wish upon a distant star*
> *What you think is what you are.*
> *It may be near, it may be far*
> *But how you live is who you are.*

Ordinary People

Sugar Ray Leonard and Thomas "Hit Man" Hearns faced each other in a widely publicized, sold-out, championship title fight June 12, 1989, at Caesar's Palace in Las Vegas, Nevada. Since I was in Las Vegas already, attending the annual Southern Baptist Convention as a messenger, I decided to try to get a ticket to the prize fight. So off I went to Caesar's Palace. Outside, throngs of people pushed and shoved to secure the best position to see the television and movie stars as they arrived for the big event. Soon, I, too, had joined the eager crowd in stargazing.

With each stretch limousine's arrival, in unison we'd stretch our necks for a glimpse of the rich and famous. I never did get a ticket to the sold-out title fight, but the stargazing was almost as much fun—and much more educational.

I soon realized that I did not know many of the arrivals. Moreover, neither did anyone else. Why? Because ordinary people, like you and me, were paying Hollywood prices for a chauffeured limousine to trumpet their arrival at Caesar's Palace. Many of these ordinary people apparently did not even have a ticket to the fight. However, they desperately needed to feel important. They craved the recognition of others. So, as they stepped out of their rented limousines, wearing rented tuxedos or rented gowns, we all strained to see the self-announced stars, elegantly attired, complete with Hollywood-style sunglasses, going nowhere.

We all want to feel important, don't we?

God so loved the world that he gave his only Son. (John 3:16a)

What's Cookin'?

Cookin' is sacred in the South. Liberation has only partially hit here. I mean, men might grill a steak, burn a burger, fry some catfish occasionally, but that's about it. The women-folk control the stove.

Things are changing some today, but not that much. A woman's identity is still, in part, tied to her ability or inability to cook. Word gets out. People talk. "Bless her heart. She stares at that stove like a calf looking at a new gate."

Twenty years ago Kay and I were newlyweds living in our native Mississippi. It was important to Kay as a young bride that she prove to be a good cook, at least as good as my mother, and who knows, in time maybe even better.

Southern gentleman image aside, sometimes we good ol' boys down South look and act less like Colonel Sanders in white and more like Gomer Pyle in grease. Not good. First month of marriage this redneck country boy blew it. How Bad? Bad, bad.

I came home from work one day, and Kay met me at the door crying. My heart sunk. "What's the matter, Honey?" I begged. "Are you okay? What's wrong, Sugar? Tell me." "Oh Honey," she broke down, "the meatloaf." She wept uncontrollably. "The dog ate the meatloaf I cooked for supper." My heart broke for her. I reached out, hugged her tight, and said, "Oh, I'm so sorry. Don't worry, Honey. I'll buy you another dog."

Those who guard their mouths preserve their lives. (Proverbs 13:3a)

Angels Attract

One early spring morning, moments before daybreak, an angel on assignment tiptoed lightly throughout the earth, carrying in her soft right hand a golden pail. In her bucket she carried love and encouragement. Her assignment? To sprinkle a little here and a little there, upon this one and that one, until every one of God's precious creations had received a gift from the golden pail, a gift of love and encouragement, to be used in blessing others when the Creator could not be present. As the celestial messenger neared the sleeping baby, Patricia Kay Donahoe, she tripped, lost her balance, and spilt the entire bucket upon the unsuspecting child. What the child could not have known, we could not have missed . . . not if we ever knew Kay.

He gave gifts to his people. (Ephesians 4:8b)